A New Religion in Mecca

Memoir of a Renegade
Brewery in St. Louis

Tom Schlafly

Copyright © 2006 Thomas F. Schlafly

ISBN: 1-891442-42-2 • $18.95

Library of Congress Control Number: 2006931829

Editor: Fran Levy
Cover designed by Alejandra Ponce de León
Book designed by Ben Pierce
Photograph layout by Ulrike Schlafly

Printed in the United States of America

Virginia Publishing Company
PO Box 4538
St. Louis, MO 63108
www.STL-Books.com

TABLE OF CONTENTS

Foreword by Bill McClellan

To Dan Kopman, who suggested that I write this book, and to Ulrike, who put up with me while I did.

FOREWORD
by Bill McClellan

If business books are not your cup of tea—and if the thought of a cup of tea does nothing for you, anyway—you ought not be confused into thinking that Tom Schlafly's book about his unlikely and successful venture into the business of beer is really a book about business. Or about beer, for that matter.

Beer and business are jumping-off points and lead into many a literary and philosophical side street. It's a bit like sharing a Pale Ale or three with a lively companion. You're not always sure where the conversation is going, but you don't care. What might start out as a story about the Missouri Legislature turns into a discourse about a beer-purity law in Bavaria in 1516, and then comes back home with a story about a similar decree in 1268 by King Louis IX of France. That's our king. The man for whom this city is named issued a consumer protection law for beer drinkers.

Not that everybody likes beer, your companion mentions. He starts talking about Prohibition, and an incident in Maplewood in which a government agent was charged with assault for shooting a patron during a saloon bust, and, by the way, did you know that Elijah Craig, a Baptist preacher from Kentucky, is widely credited with having first produced bourbon? The relative who took over that family's brewery business in New York was Matthew Vassar. He, too, was a Baptist, and he founded Vassar College. That heritage is recalled in the popular Vassar song that ends: "Full well we know that all we owe to Matthew Vassar's ale."

These days, they sing of what they owe to Matthew Vassar's "aid," but in the original version, it was his ale, your friend assures you.

You sip your Pale Ale, and you think, "How does he know all of this?"

That's Schlafly, though. A Renaissance Man. He's a lawyer, businessman, National Public Radio commentator, singer-satirist and essayist. Now he's an author. Just the kind of man who'd name his beer after himself. But wait. There is a story behind that.

What would you name your beer? Names that were considered included Louis IX, Pierre Laclede, Lewis & Clark, Daniel Boone, Mark

Twain, Jesse James, Catfish, Channel Cat, Osage, Steamboat and Limestone. But if you put your family name on the beer, you're sending the message that you're staking your reputation on the quality of the beer. That makes sense.

If names are important, so are labels. Here's an insight: You don't want your label to be too upscale. Yuppies will buy products with a blue-collar image, but blue-collar workers will balk at buying products with a yuppie image. That might seem like a little thing, but if you're going to beat the odds and successfully start a brewery in the shadow of the world's largest brewery, you have to get everything right.

In a way, then, this book is about business. And about beer, too. Happily, it just doesn't read that way.

THE STRONG BROWN GOD

You have to be careful if you don't know where you're going,
because you might not get there.

The wisdom of St. Louis native Yogi Berra, so apt for so many situations, certainly applies to Schlafly Beer. Back in 1991, I really had no idea where we were going. Fifteen years later, in 2006, I honestly don't know whether we ever actually got there.

That said, we would appear to be in pretty good company. Some of the most famous journeys in history have led somewhere other than the intended destinations. In 1492, Christopher Columbus set sail from Palos on the Gulf of Cadiz, hoping to reach India. When he landed on an island in the Bahamas, he thought he was in Asia and claimed the land for the King of Spain. Later, upon reaching Cuba, Columbus was convinced he had found Japan.

One hundred twenty-eight years later, in 1620, Pilgrims on the *Mayflower* left England with the intention of landing in the northern part of the Virginia colony, in what is now New York State. Instead they found themselves in New England. According to William Bradford, the Governor of Plymouth Colony, the Pilgrims decided to come ashore on December 19 in part because they were running low on beer ("our victuals being much spent, especially our beer").

One hundred eighty-four years later, on May 14, 1804, Meriwether Lewis and William Clark left Camp River Dubois, just north of St. Louis, along with their Corps of Discovery, hoping to discover the fabled "River of the West," or Northwest Passage, that would take them to the Pacific Ocean. After traveling more than 8,000 miles, they returned to St. Louis on September 23, 1806, with the unwelcome news that the much-touted Northwest Passage did not exist.

The journey of Schlafly Beer is both similar to and different from those of Columbus, the Pilgrims and Lewis and Clark. Like these famous travelers, when we first embarked we weren't really sure where we were going. Unlike them, our journey has already lasted 15 years and we still have no idea what our final destination is. By contrast, the Pilgrims' renowned voyage took a mere four and a half months; and the period from start to finish of the Lewis and Clark expedition was only 27 months. All four voyages of Christopher Columbus took place within a span of 12 years.

How did we get to where we are today? Where, in fact, are we headed? I might begin to answer these questions by quoting another St. Louis native, T. S. Eliot, who wrote in *The Dry Salvages*:

I do not know much about gods; but I think that the river
Is a strong brown god—sullen, untamed and intractable…
His rhythm was present in the nursery bedroom.

Eliot's nursery bedroom was on Locust Street near Jefferson, in the City of St. Louis, three blocks west of The Schlafly Tap Room. The river to which he refers, the Mississippi, is an apt metaphor for this narrative. The story I am about to tell is one that meanders as unpredictably as the Mississippi or any other sullen, untamed and intractable river.

In choosing to tell the story in this fashion, I am not succumbing to authorial laziness. There's simply no other way to tell it. Our history is not one that lends itself to orderly, logical, chronological presentation. Just as the Mississippi periodically overflows its banks, rises and falls according to its own whims, seeks new channels when it tires of existing ones and blithely disregards human efforts to manage and contain it, so too has Schlafly Beer constantly charted new courses for itself, seemingly oblivious to every business plan we have so conscientiously written to appease our bankers.

Beer is indeed a strong brown god, a beverage with its own deities in the ancient religions of Sumeria and Egypt (Ninkasi and Tenenit, respectively). Like the Mississippi, beer can be frustratingly independent for the humans who would seek to master it. Even though beer has been around longer than the wheel, explanations for some of what takes place during the brewing process can still prove annoyingly elusive to the best scientists in the world. Perhaps it was inevitable that a business built around brewing would be as unpredictable as the beverage at its core. And just as much fun.

In many ways our history resembles a jazz performance, jazz being a genre that is commonly associated with St. Louis and reflects the characteristics of the river whose valley nurtured it. Like the Mississippi, jazz is sullen, untamed and intractable. It is not carefully orchestrated like a symphony, the success of which depends on each musician's doing exactly what he or she is supposed to do at precisely the right point in the performance. The genius of jazz is in improvisation. When a pianist plays a note, he or she often has no idea what note will follow. Whatever note it might be, the trumpet player and the saxophonist must both be prepared to use it as the starting point for solos of their own.

The history of Schlafly Beer has involved a lot more improvisation than careful orchestration. At times it seems that we're almost like a football team that runs nothing but busted plays. While some might decry our apparent inability to follow a business plan, I am convinced that we would not have survived for 15 years if we weren't able to adapt to changing and unforeseen circumstances. Put another way, when opportunities we had never imagined have presented themselves, we have, fortunately, been flexible and nimble enough to take advantage of them.

We have also been extraordinarily lucky. In countless instances, we have made the right decisions for the wrong reasons. We have been blissfully ignorant of some dangers that could have been very real. We have attracted some very talented employees without necessarily seeking them out. And we have declined to make some decisions that could have been catastrophic, not fully appreciating at the time how disastrous the consequences would have been.

In one sense, the series of improbable circumstances that led to the founding of The Saint Louis Brewery began in 1977, when I graduated from law school and was hired by a firm in which Charles Kopman was a partner. At the time, Charles's son, Dan, was still in high school. Although Charles left the firm in 1980, while Dan was in college, Charles and I continued to bump into each other from time to time.

At one of these serendipitous encounters, perhaps in 1983, I happened to mention to Charles that I had recently been to England and had enjoyed the "real ale" in some English pubs. I added that it was too bad such beers weren't more commonly available in the United States. Charles replied that his son Dan, whom I barely remembered, had graduated from college and was working for a British brewery. His job consisted of traveling throughout the world, selling beers like those I had enjoyed in England.

Somehow this casual conversation led to more serious discussions among Charles, Dan and me. Whenever Dan's business brought him to St. Louis, the three of us would meet for lunch to talk about a phenomenon that Dan had seen in other parts of the country: microbreweries. Because beers from these breweries were often sold through the same wholesalers that carried beers from Young's, the London brewery for which Dan was working, he had an opportunity to observe the growth of this segment in a lot of local markets. At every single lunch, Dan's message was the same, "Microbreweries are a concept that will work in St. Louis." And my response was always the same, "St. Louis is different from these other markets."

As anyone who has met him can attest, Dan is a very persistent salesman. After several years of meeting every few months, he finally convinced me that there was a market for craft beer in St. Louis. Our goal would not be to compete with the large breweries. Rather, we would brew the styles that they didn't offer, a universe that potentially included hundreds of different beers.

On August 22, 1989, I took the first step of incorporating The Saint Louis Brewery, Inc. The initial shareholders who still own stock in the company, in addition to me, included Charles Kopman, Dan Kopman and Joe Tennant, a law school classmate from Portland, Oregon.

After looking at what had failed and succeeded in other markets, we decided to start by opening a brewpub, a small brewery that would sell the beer it brewed at a restaurant on the same premises. This decision was influenced by a number of considerations, including legal restrictions, which will be discussed in greater detail in Chapter 4. The main reason, however, was our realization that we needed a location to help people identify with the beer. With a restaurant, customers would associate the beer with a place they had visited and where they had had a pleasant experience (we hoped), much like a winery in a scenic setting.

Initially we thought the main focus of the establishment would be on beer, with food being secondary or incidental. Charles and I, in particular, wanted to keep our involvement in the restaurant business to an absolute minimum, having seen many restaurants fail in our years of practicing law. As I shall explain a little later on, we were lucky that we were persuaded to overcome our skittishness.

The first location that we seriously considered for our brewpub was a former mortuary in Grand Center, an entertainment district in midtown St. Louis. The building had a lot of attractive features, but parking presented a major problem. It dawned on us that when the St. Louis Symphony was performing or when there was a touring Broadway show at the nearby

Fox Theatre, our potential restaurant customers wouldn't be able to find a place to park, at least not at a price they'd be willing to pay. The busier the various entertainment venues were, the harder it would be for our patrons to find free parking, which was and is almost a prerequisite for St. Louisans wanting a simple meal and a pint of beer.

Although we didn't put our brewpub in Grand Center, our investigation of the area led us to the architect and contractor who later built our brewery for us. Proving either that the beer gods—including the Sumerian goddess Ninkasi and the Egyptian god Tenenit—were, in fact, smiling on our venture, or that dumb luck is an opportunity for improvisation that must be seized in a timely manner, it was through Grand Center that we met an architect named Tom Cohen; and it was through Tom that we met a contractor named Anne Wotka, who was also his ex-wife. (Trust me, I am not making this up.) Although their marriage didn't last, the business relationship did.

The next location that we seriously considered was a former Union Electric substation (Union Electric being the predecessor to AmerenUE, the electric utility company that now serves St. Louis). It was located slightly north of Washington Avenue, not far from what later became the City Museum. It was also across the street from the former International Shoe Building, where Tennessee Williams had worked with a man named Stanley Kowalski, who served as the model for the character played by Marlon Brando in A *Streetcar Named Desire*.

In 1991, this neighborhood did not look at all promising, that being one of the reasons the building was in our price range. Many of the nearby buildings were vacant and in need of extensive repair. There never seemed to be anyone on the street. When a real estate agent optimistically praised the neighborhood as "cutting edge," we laughed and marveled at his ability to keep a straight face while putting such positive spin on such a hopeless situation.

Fifteen years later, his description has proved to have been more prescient than Dan or I ever would have imagined. The club scene on Washington Avenue and demand for residential lofts in the area have indeed made this "cutting edge" neighborhood one of the bigger success stories in St. Louis.

The former substation was owned by a lawyer who expressed great eagerness to have us as his tenant. Whenever, in the course of our negotiations, I pointed out some potential problems, such as insufficient fire exits, he always assured me that he could arrange to get zoning variances. As he continued to press us to sign a lease, I finally drafted one and incorporated all the promises he had made as terms of the lease. I included language that said that if the representations he had made were not correct—e.g., we weren't able to get the zoning variances he had promised—the lease was void.

The lawyer indignantly refused to sign the lease and directed various threats and insults toward Dan and me. He subsequently filed a lawsuit against us seeking three years' rent on the building we hadn't rented. He supported his lawsuit with an affidavit full of false statements. Fortunately, the court ruled in favor of our motion for summary judgment, meaning that even if he were telling the truth—he wasn't—he still didn't have a case. Once again, the beer gods had interceded on our behalf. Had we had this man as a landlord, I doubt very much that our business could have survived.

At this point, Anne Wotka, who, like Cassandra, had been incessantly warning us about the lawyer, started insisting vigorously that we buy the John S. Swift Building at 2100 Locust Street, the former home of Swift Printing Company. It was a beautiful structure, listed on the National Register of Historic Places, but it had fallen on hard times. Swift had moved out in 1969, 22 years earlier, and the intervening years had not been kind. In addition to the predations that typically befall any vacant building in an urban area, the Swift Building had suffered extensive damage in a huge firestorm that had engulfed the neighborhood in 1976. In the intervening years, the building's main claim to fame had been a cameo role in *Escape from New York*, John Carpenter's 1981 film starring Kurt Russell as Snake Plissken.

When Dan and I protested that the Swift Building was too big and we couldn't afford to renovate it, Anne invariably replied with an extremely colorful epithet and said, "Don't worry. Just buy the damn building. Whatever you can afford to pay, I'll get the project done for that amount." In the end, it was a lot easier to acquiesce than to argue with her. We bought the building on July 17, 1991. Anne and her crew went to work immediately and, as promised, we were able to have our grand opening five months later, on December 26. As had happened in the past, the beer gods were again looking out for us.

Unfortunately, Anne died on the job suddenly and unexpectedly on January 25, 1995. Characteristically, when she breathed her final breath, she was working hard at what she loved to do and did so well. We were tremendously honored that her family and friends chose to have a memorial celebration of her life at The Tap Room. We absolutely would not be where we are if it weren't for her. And we were genuinely touched that those close to her thought she would want to be remembered for having built The Tap Room.

By the time we decided to buy the Swift Building, we had also amended our thinking about the restaurant. It was Susan Katzman, a professional restaurant consultant, who convinced us that a bar with minimal food service, which is what Dan, Charles and I favored, simply would not work. While she sympathized with our desire to minimize our risk by offering only microwaved sandwiches, soups and pizza along with beer, she was able to explain to us why this approach was seriously flawed. In essence, she said, "Your food sends a message about your beer. If you don't care about the quality of the food, your customers will think you don't care about the quality of your beer either."

With Susan's input, we have consistently and successfully offered a distinctive menu at The Tap Room. Thanks in large part to our willingness to listen to her advice, there are patrons who, while uninterested or indifferent to the selection of beers on tap, will happily travel great distances for our white bean chili, fish and fries or ploughman's plate.

It was Susan who recommended Tom Flood, our first restaurant manager. In addition to helping to set the tone at The Tap Room for years to come, Tom also has the distinction of having resigned from The Saint Louis Brewery, Inc., more frequently than any other employee (five times as of the date this manuscript was sent to the printer).

I still remember the time I ordered Tom to attend the wedding of one of our cooks. I told him very authoritatively that if I went to the wedding, he had to go also. "No, I don't." "Damn it, Flood. He works for you. If you don't go to the wedding, you're fired!" "O.K. Fire me." Of course he knew as well as I did that I wouldn't follow through on my empty threat.

The cast of characters from the early days also includes Jeff Wamhoff, an employee of the St. Louis Art Museum who built the magnificent bar in the south dining room at The Tap Room. As far as I know, this was the second connection between our building and the Art Museum, the first being Samuel Sherer, the architect who originally designed the building and went on to serve as the Director of the Art Museum in the 1920s.

Paul Jensen, our most senior bartender, started with us before we opened and is the longest-serving of all of our employees. Interestingly, his previous job, before joining us, was with the Anheuser-Busch wholesaler in Houston.

At the same time that we hired Paul, we also hired Tom Sweeney, who had extensive experience in the restaurant business. Tom had unrivaled skills when it came to dealing with dissatisfied customers. But even he couldn't defuse every situation. Shortly after we opened, with the paint barely dry on the walls, a disgruntled patron, without apparent provocation, slammed Tom into the wall and put a hole in our brand new drywall. It was at that point that Dan Kopman turned to me and said, "Well, Tom, welcome to the bar business."

Someone who did not have a lot of experience in the restaurant business, or work experience of any kind in his mid-forties, was Dave Miller, our first brewer. Dave's wife worked for the federal government and, before coming to work for us, he was a stay-at-home dad who took care of their five children and wrote books about home brewing. He showed up for his job interview in a Boy Scout uniform with short pants, having just come from a field trip to the Gateway Arch with a pack of Cub Scouts.

Dave had a candor that could be both endearing and unsettling, as was demonstrated the time he answered the phone and then yelled across a dining room full of patrons, "Hey, Dan. There's a guy calling about the asbestos in the basement." For the record, I want to emphasize that the asbestos situation to which he was referring has been fully abated.

Dave's first assistant brewer was Stephen Hale, who had majored in Classics at Kenyon College, where he had met Dan. Stephen was an amateur brewer whose professional experience included sweeping chimneys and diving for sea urchins. He started with us in 1991, but has not been with us continuously, having spent the summer of 1994 working for a brewery in Maine. As I have often told him, when it got hot in St. Louis, he moved to Maine. When it got cold in Maine, he moved back to St. Louis.

Looking back, I truly am amazed that we were able to open for business as quickly as we did. Part of the building was in such bad shape that it was possible to stand in the basement and see daylight through the roof, three stories up. We had no brewery, no kitchen and no equipment or fixtures of any kind. Moreover, many of us had little or no experience relevant to what we were about to do.

We were fortunate in that the inevitable delays almost seemed coordinated with each other. The delays in the delivery of kitchen equipment were about the same as the delays in the delivery of brewing equipment, which were about the same as the construction delays, which were about the same as the delays in getting the requisite permits and licenses etc. Everything was ready at about the same time and we didn't have to pay for anything too far ahead of when we needed it.

We had wanted to be open in time for Christmas and almost made it. After a few trial runs with the restaurant, we had our grand opening on Thursday, December 26, 1991. We served free beer and home-made pretzels and attracted a huge crowd that included brewers from Anheuser-Busch, politicians and a lot of people who simply couldn't believe that anyone would dare to open another brewery in St. Louis, with some of my friends and close relatives numbered among the greatest skeptics.

A few weeks later, on a Friday night in January of 1992, we discovered that we had miscalculated. While we thought we had brewed an adequate supply of beer, we realized that we were going to run out before the next batch was ready to be tapped. Shortly before midnight, Dan stood on the bar and announced to a crowded room, "I'm terribly sorry, but we've run out of beer."

The reaction among the patrons was not the disappointment or anger he had anticipated. Instead, a spontaneous, triumphant chant arose, "We drank 'em dry! We drank 'em dry! We drank 'em dry!"

Like the Pilgrims on the Mayflower in 1620, we knew we had to do something. Dan ordered an emergency shipment of Bully Porter from Boulevard Brewery in Kansas City, which carried us over until the next batch of Schlafly Wheat Ale was ready to serve.

A NEW RELIGION IN MECCA

The Ayatollah drinks Coors.

This was the message proclaimed by a bumper sticker on an American-made automobile in South St. Louis in 1980. I'm sure the owner of the vehicle could think of nothing worse to say either about the Ayatollah or about Coors. The Ayatollah Ruhollah Khomeini was the Shiite cleric who had proclaimed himself Supreme Leader of Iran and was the public face of the regime that was holding 63 Americans hostage in the U. S. Embassy in Tehran. Coors was the beer from Colorado that was trying to make inroads into St. Louis, Anheuser-Busch's home town. In the words of another bumper sticker from the same time: "Coors, non-union, non-pasteurized." The fact that Coors wasn't brewed in St. Louis was bad enough. That the brewery wasn't unionized made it all the more execrable.

I wondered at the time whether the owner of the car had considered the comical incongruity of the image of a fervently devout Muslim drinking any kind of beer in the face of the strict Islamic prohibition against alcoholic beverages. It then occurred to me that forbidding beer is but one of several tenets shared by Muslims and Mormons, two groups that are otherwise not generally associated with each other.

Both were founded by polygamists (Mohammed having had at least 30 wives, Joseph Smith at least 50) and have tolerated polygamy among their adherents. Both denominations split in their respective early days over the issue of leadership and bloodlines. (The Shiite minority believe that the leader of Islam must be descended from the Prophet Mohammed. The Reorganized Church of Jesus Christ of Latter Day Saints, whose members stayed in Independence, Missouri, instead of trekking to Utah, was traditionally led by a descendant of Joseph Smith.) And finally, each denomination has its headquarters in a desert (in Mecca and Salt Lake City, respectively).

St. Louis is very different from Mecca and Salt Lake City in both culture and geography. The prevalence and wide acceptance of beer in the city are totally incompatible with the dictates of the *Koran* and *Mormon Doctrine and Covenants*. And the city's location at the confluence of the two greatest rivers in North America, the Missouri and the Mississippi, offers an abundance of fresh water that makes the region the antithesis of a desert. As might be expected, the geography of St. Louis is largely responsible for its culture.

In 1824, a German attorney named Gottfried Duden settled near what is now the town of Dutzow, west of St. Louis on the Missouri River. He was so impressed by the area that he returned to Germany and in 1829 published *Eine Reise zu den westlichen Staaten von Nordamerika* (A Journey to the Western States of North America). This glowing account prompted a wave of German immigration to Missouri, starting in the 1830s.

The failed German revolution of 1848 caused more Germans to emigrate, with many of the so-called "Forty-Eighters" finding their way to St. Louis. Among them was Franz Sigel, a graduate of Karlsruhe Military Academy and one of the few revolutionaries with military command experience. Like most Forty-Eighters, he was very much opposed to slavery. And, like many of his fellow immigrants, Sigel fought with the Union Army during the Civil War. Many historians, in fact, credit the progressive Forty-Eighters with keeping Missouri, a slave state, from joining the Confederacy.

These German immigrants came to St. Louis with a taste not just for freedom, but also for beer. Once again the city's geography was very helpful. First, there was an abundance of good water, which makes up more than 90 percent of beer. Second, there was an extensive network of underground limestone caves, with year-round temperatures in the 50s, making them ideal for storing beer.

Adam Lemp, a German immigrant who may have been inspired by Gottfried Duden, is credited by some with having brewed the first lager beer in the United Sates, perhaps as early as 1838. Whether Lemp in fact started brewing this early, it's generally accepted that by 1842 he had built a large commercial brewery that was primarily producing lager beer, the style most common in the United States today.

It was 18 years later, in 1860, that Eberhard Anheuser acquired sole possession of the Bavarian Brewery, which had gone bankrupt. The following year, his daughter Lilly married Adolphus Busch, a partner in a firm that sold brewing supplies. In 1865 Adolphus purchased an interest in the brewery, which was then brewing 4,000 barrels per year, far less than the Lemp brewery. Upon the death of Eberhard Anheuser in 1880, Adolphus assumed ownership of the brewery, now known as Anheuser-Busch. This was four years after the brewery had started selling a beer called Budweiser, named for a town in what is now the Czech Republic.

Anheuser-Busch continued to grow under the leadership of Adolphus Busch, who died in 1913, prior to the outbreak of the First World War and the subsequent adoption of the 18th Amendment to the United States Constitution. The war fueled a wave of viciously anti-German sentiment, which proponents of Prohibition exploited by pointing to the German ancestry and alleged disloyalty of the so-called "beer barons." When Prohibition became the law of the land in 1920, Anheuser-Busch, with August A. Busch as president, was one of only 583 breweries in the United States, down from 1,771 in 1900. (August Sr. had the additional distinction of having been one of the honorary pallbearers at the funeral of my great-grandfather William C. McBride, who died in 1917, shortly after the United States entered the war against Germany.)

The Lemp Brewery, which had dominated the St. Louis market, shut down permanently with the advent of Prohibition. Not long thereafter, in 1922, William Lemp, Jr., the last president of the brewery, committed suicide. Twelve years later, in 1934, after the ratification of the 21st Amendment, which repealed Prohibition, August A. Busch, whose brewery had survived the brewing industry's darkest hour, also killed himself.

Although a lot of breweries, like Lemp, failed to reopen after the repeal of Prohibition; and there was a lot of consolidation in the industry for reasons other than Prohibition, there were still several local breweries in St. Louis following the Second World War. A picture of Sportsman's Park during the 1946 World Series between the Cardinals and the Red Sox shows signs in the stadium for Hyde Park, Alpen Brau, Falstaff and Griesedieck Brothers, as well as bottles of Budweiser offered by a vendor in the stands. A slogan that was popular at the time proclaimed that St. Louis was "first in shoes, first in booze and last in the American League." Things soon changed.

In 1953, August A. Busch, Jr., popularly known as "Gussie," was president of the brewery and made the decision to buy the St. Louis Cardinals. In 1954, the St. Louis Browns, perhaps the most feckless team in baseball, moved to Baltimore and transformed themselves into the Orioles. It's an interesting bit of sports trivia (at least interesting to some of us) that the two professional sports teams now playing in Baltimore, i.e., the Ravens and Orioles, were both called the "Browns" in their former homes, Cleveland and St. Louis, respectively.

While St. Louis abruptly shed the dubious distinction of being last in the American League, the loss of dominance in shoes was far more gradual, as production moved overseas. With respect to beer, on the other hand, the city's dominance continued to grow, thanks entirely to Anheuser-Busch. A-B's annual production, which had reached the milestone of one million barrels in 1901, was at 10 million barrels in 1964. By 2005, the brewery's annual production had increased more than tenfold, to nearly 117 million barrels, giving it roughly half of the American market. Meanwhile, the other brands of beer offered at the 1946 World Series have been reduced to mere historical footnotes.

In the midst of this consolidation, there was a bold local forerunner to the craft beer movement. In the late 1960s, Van Dyke Brewery was brewing in St. Charles, slightly west of St. Louis. Its most memorable legacy today might well be its commercials, which reportedly encouraged customers to "take a case of VD home to your wife."

As Anheuser-Busch's production and market share increased, so did its cultural presence in St. Louis. After purchasing the Cardinals, the new owners changed the name of their ballpark from Sportsman's Park, which had been home to both the Cardinals and the Browns, to Busch Stadium. This was the same name given to the stadium where the team played from 1966 to 2005, as well as that of the new ballpark, which opened for the 2006 season. Baseball historians have noted that the Cardinals are the only team to have played home games in three different stadiums, all with the same name.

It wasn't just the name on the outside of the stadium that distinguished the home of the Cardinals. Inside the park it was virtually, if not completely, impossible to purchase beers not brewed by Anheuser-Busch. The song made famous by its use in Budweiser commercials ("When You Say Bud") was heard more often than "Take Me Out to the Ballgame." While it played, fans stood and applauded a video of Clydesdales pulling a Budweiser wagon. On special occasions, such as Opening Day or the first home game of the World Series, Gussie Busch himself would ride into the stadium on the Clydesdale wagon.

When he did, the reaction of the crowd was one typically reserved for royalty in European countries. I vividly recall seeing fans in the bleachers, who probably weren't earning too much more than the minimum wage, anxiously looking for a vendor in order to buy a beer with which to toast Gussie when his wagon went by. These guys readily and willingly paid close to what they earned in an hour for a cup of beer, happily putting more money into the pockets of the billionaire on the horse-drawn wagon.

Anheuser-Busch had, and still has, a status unlike that of any other corporation based in St. Louis. While other large companies are known by their official names, A-B is simply called "The Brewery." No one ever called McDonnell-Douglass (now Boeing) "The Aircraft Company." No one ever refers to Monsanto as "The Chemical Company." Pulitzer was never "The Publishing Company." Even the media accept this convention. Traffic reports almost invariably refer to the congestion, or lack thereof, "on I-55 by The Brewery."

This was the climate when we decided to open another brewery in St. Louis. Since the closing of the Falstaff brewery in 1977, no one other than Anheuser-Busch had brewed beer commercially in St. Louis. And no one had presumed to open a new brewery in the St. Louis area since the demise of the Van Dyke operation two decades earlier. At times I compared what we were doing to opening the first Toyota dealership in Detroit. At other times I said it was like starting a new religion in Mecca.

When I first incorporated the business in 1989, we couldn't decide on a name for the beer and simply chose The Saint Louis Brewery, Inc., for the company, figuring that we could come up with a name for the beer later on (a process I'll discuss more fully in Chapter 6). This decision led to some interesting incidents when I was asked what my occupation was and I responded, "president of The Saint Louis Brewery." People then usually asked if I were a member of the Busch family, to which I replied, "No. They own the other brewery."

One of the most amusing incidents of mistaken identity didn't happen in St. Louis, but in the town of Budvar in the Czech Republic, the home of the brewery that brews the Budweiser that's sold in most of Europe. In the summer of 2001, nearly 10 years after Schlafly Beer opened for business, my wife, Ulrike, and I rented a car and drove through Germany, Austria and the Czech Republic. Through a friend in Vienna who knew the Czech Ambassador to Austria, we arranged to have a tour of the brewery in Budvar. As we soon learned, something got lost in translation as the message was relayed through various parties in English, German and Czech.

We were met at the entrance to the brewery by a very charming tour guide who led us through the various stages of the brewing process. After about 20 minutes, she said to me very pleasantly, "Now, you are the president of Anheuser-Busch, correct?" I patiently explained that I wasn't. I then noted that I doubted that the president of Anheuser-Busch would have traveled in a modest rental car full of dirty laundry; and he probably wouldn't have gotten lost on the way from Vienna to Budvar, as we had, since he probably would have had access to a better map than the one we were using.

Whenever I'm asked how it is to operate a small, upstart brewery in the shadow of The Brewery, I honestly say that there are both pluses and minuses. Among the negatives is a resistance on the part of some consumers to any beer not brewed by Anheuser-Busch, as if drinking anything else would somehow be a betrayal of a good corporate citizen in the community. There's also an unwillingness on the part of some retailers to carry any other products, with some restaurant managers adamantly declaring, "This is an A-B establishment." Period! Among the positives is the huge amount of free publicity we have received for starting another brewery. The concept was and is so unimaginable that it was, and still is, newsworthy.

When our plans were first announced, we got a lot of attention in both print and electronic media. We also benefited from the herd mentality of a lot of news outlets. If one TV station announced that it was going to cover something, it was generally pretty easy to persuade the others to follow suit, so they wouldn't miss an important story that one of their competitors was going to cover.

I soon learned that the coverage was almost always positive. The media naturally picked up the David and Goliath angle. As I once said to an employee of a public relations firm that did work for Anheuser-Busch, "Face it. There's never going to be a story about us picking on your client. The media are never going to say that we're the bad guys."

If favorable free publicity could ever amount to our having too much of a good thing, it happened to us in September of 1992, when we were planning our first Oktoberfest. We talked to a sympathetic reporter from a local TV station, which obligingly ran a story that featured footage from the Munich Oktoberfest, showing hundreds of thousands of exuberant celebrants. Within minutes we got two frantic phone calls, one from a neighboring business and one from our insurance agent. Their message was the same: "What in the hell are you people doing?" It took a while to reassure them that the Oktoberfest we were contemplating was definitely not on the same scale as that in Munich.

Throughout this time, Anheuser-Busch's reaction to our emergence could best be described as one of cautious curiosity. Prior to our official opening on December 26, 1991, I wrote a letter to August Busch, III, with a personal invitation. Someone from his office called promptly to say that Mr. Busch would not be able to attend, but he was sending Phil Colombatto, who's now the Vice President for Quality Assurance. Although I had not personally met Phil, it was easy to pick him out in the crowd, because he was the one in a Budweiser jacket, with a small glass of each of our beers, carefully eyeing, smelling and tasting each of them in turn.

August Busch, III, himself made his first (and I assume only) appearance at The Tap Room in 1993. It was preceded by at least five telephone calls from a secretary in his office, who kept trying to make reservations for lunch and was told every time that we didn't take reservations. And no, our reservation policy hadn't changed in the past five minutes. Yes, it was still the same as it was during her first, second, third and fourth calls.

When he arrived, Mr. Busch showed similar persistence in trying to order Anheuser-Busch products in the face of being told repeatedly that we sold only Schlafly Beer. Despite his disappointment, I have been told by the server who waited on him that he seemed to enjoy his lunch and left a generous tip.

The next significant visit from the largest brewery in St. Louis involved its specialty beer group, members of which had been flown in from all over the country. Presumably in order to familiarize these employees with the craft beer sector, the company brought a busload of them, first to The Tap Room for lunch and then to a winery on the Missouri River, not far from where Gottfried Duden had settled more than 165 years earlier. In all candor, I have to admit that it was tremendously flattering to think that people at A-B thought they could learn anything from us.

In 1995, something happened that most St. Louisans had considered unthinkable. Anheuser-Busch announced that it was selling the Cardinals. I heard the news from Christine Bertelson, who was then a columnist for the *St. Louis Post-Dispatch*. Somehow our conversation led to her writing a playful column in which she jokingly speculated about our buying the team. As often happens, the story took on a life of its own. I struggled to keep a straight face during interviews when I told journalists from out of town that I was serious about wanting to buy the team.

We put a jar on the bar to collect donations to help us finance the purchase. Then we drew a graph on a chalkboard to show how the campaign was going. "Amount needed: Over $150 million. Amount raised to date: $134." An unidentified employee added the helpful observation, "This could take a while." When the team was later sold to the investors who currently own it, we donated what was in the jar to the *St. Louis Post-Dispatch 100 Neediest Cases*, along with a matching additional contribution of our own.

One of the consequences of the sale of the Cardinals was a slightly more permissive attitude toward serving non-Anheuser-Busch beers at the ballpark. For the start of the 1997 season, there were two Schlafly taps in Busch Stadium, a development that some observers had considered inconceivable. In later years, Schlafly would be offered in bottles at two additional locations in the park. The new Busch Stadium, which opened in 2006, has two taps with draft Schlafly and several other locations where bottled Schlafly is sold.

While getting our beer into Busch Stadium in 1997 was a real milestone, what happened at Grant's Farm two years earlier was far more dramatic. The occasion was a dinner party hosted by Trudy Busch, Gussie's former wife, at the magnificent family estate now owned by their children. It was in June of 1995, and Ulrike and I, who had just become engaged, were among those invited to the party. After dinner, Trudy mentioned in passing that it was a shame everyone couldn't toast our engagement with Schlafly Beer. I replied that I happened to have some in a cooler in my car. Trudy then told a waiter to get the beer from my trunk and serve it to all the guests.

At least one of those in attendance thought that what had happened was so extraordinary that it warranted reporting in the newspaper. I have been told that the story that appeared in the *St. Louis Post-Dispatch* a few days later caused considerable consternation at One Busch Place, where rent checks were and are being written to the family for the brewery's use of Grant's Farm.

We hadn't just started a new religion in Mecca. Now we were proselytizing in the Grand Mosque.

THE IDEA OF A UNIVERSITY

> *And malt does more than Milton can*
> *To justify God's ways to man.*

These lines were written by A. E. Housman in "A Shropshire Lad," which I studied while majoring in English at Georgetown University. The message at the time seemed to me to be pretty clear. I could learn more over a pitcher of beer at the Tombs, a student hangout near the campus, than I could by reading *Paradise Lost* in the library. Fortuitously, at the time, the legal drinking age in the District of Columbia for beer and wine was 18, as opposed to 21 for hard liquor, making it that much easier to follow a Shropshire lad's example in education.

The Tombs wasn't the only venue where I pursued my undergraduate beer studies. Matt Kane's Bit o' Ireland, which featured Irish music, was where I had my first taste of Irish stout. And it was the Old Stein, on Connecticut Avenue near Dupont Circle, where my classmates and I discovered imported German beer.

Thirteen years after receiving my undergraduate degree from Georgetown, I embarked on additional beer studies at Oxford University in the summer of 1983. By this time, I was a lawyer in private practice in St. Louis, having also received my law degree at Georgetown in 1977. I had enrolled in a continuing legal education course at St. Edmund's Hall at Oxford, the subject of which was a comparison of the English and American legal systems. Perhaps under the lingering influence of A. E. Housman, who had studied at St. John's College, Oxford, I learned a lot more about English beer than I did about English law.

My introduction to Oxford was at The Bear, a traditional pub not far from St. Edmund's (a.k.a. Teddy Hall), where part of my necktie was clipped off and added to the collection on the ceiling. I later ventured farther from Teddy Hall to The Trout and The Perch, both well worth the walk from town on a pleasant summer evening. At these and other establishments that I frequented during my time at Oxford, the drink of choice was always "real ale," which was served at cellar temperature from the cask in which it had been conditioned. It suddenly dawned on me that these very ales were the answer to the question posed by A. E. Housman in "A Shropshire Lad":

> *Say, for what were hop-yards meant,*
> *Or why was Burton built on Trent?*

Shortly after I returned from my Oxonian sojourn, my palate awakened and my horizons expanded, I had the propitious encounter with Charles Kopman, who told me about his son Dan's job with Young's.

When I recount my experiences at Georgetown and Oxford (seven years at the former, two weeks at the latter), I am sometimes asked whether I think I spent a lot of time on things that were essentially trivial. Drawing once again on my experience as an English major, I always delight in quoting James Joyce: "Yes, trivial and quadrivial." (Joyce, who was responding to a question about whether the puns in *Finnegan's Wake* were "trivial," was referring to the *trivium* and the *quadrivium*, which collectively comprised the seven traditional liberal arts.)

In the Middle Ages, the liberal arts (*artes liberales*), formed the basis of educating the free man (*liber* being the Latin word for "free") in his pursuit of knowledge for the sake of knowledge, as opposed to the illiberal arts (*artes illiberales*), which were studied for mere economic purposes. Among the liberal arts, the *artes triviales*, or *trivium*, consisted of grammar, rhetoric and logic; and the *artes quadriviales*, or *quadrivium*, consisted of arithmetic, geometry, astronomy and music. As universities began to spring up around Europe, it was said, "Universitas fundatur in artibus." (The university has its foundation in the arts.)

When we founded The Saint Louis Brewery, we seemed to attract people steeped in liberal arts. Faithful to the medieval preference for *artes liberales* over *artes illiberales*, almost no one had had any training that could be considered practical or useful when it came to operating a brewery. I, as I have said, had majored in English, as had Dave Miller, our first head brewer. Dan Kopman had majored in economics at Kenyon College, a fascinating discipline that is of no use whatsoever when it comes to setting up a spreadsheet. Stephen Hale, who succeeded Dave as head brewer, had majored in Classics at Kenyon, studying perhaps the most liberal of the *artes liberales*. His wife, Sara, our first head of quality control, had majored in fine arts at the University of Kansas. And James Ottolini (Otto) became our chief engineer after majoring in French, also at Kansas.

In all fairness, so as not to understate anyone's qualifications, I should note that Dan and Stephen had learned about home brewing at Kenyon from Perry Lentz, a professor in the English Department. Also, when Dan spent his junior year abroad at the University of Edinburgh, he wrote his thesis on "The Economic History of the British Brewing Industry." Finally, as I'll discuss in greater detail in the next chapter, Charles Kopman's and my legal educations have been an unfortunate necessity from the outset.

While a university education (whether in the liberal or illiberal arts) is revered throughout the world, what really matters in St. Louis is where one went to high school. For reasons that are self-evident to those of us who grew up in St. Louis—and utterly bewildering to those who didn't— St. Louisans are renowned for asking, within minutes of meeting someone, "Where did you go to high school?" The answer invariably provides the equivalent of several chapters of relevant biography. At the same time, not knowing where someone went to high school can leave an unexplained gap in the individual's résumé that makes St. Louisans very uncomfortable.

St. Louis Priory School, my alma mater, is relatively new (the first class graduated in 1960, the year I entered seventh grade), but has a tradition that extends back nearly 1,500 years to the founding of the Benedictines, the order of monks who run the school. Although reading this might horrify some of the monks who taught me, their Benedictine influence is at least partially responsible for my getting into the beer business.

Priory virtually ensured that I would study liberal arts in college, an apparent prerequisite for working for Schlafly Beer. I took six years of Latin, six years of French, three years of Greek and a lot of other subjects that some would consider impractical. I wasn't even aware of the *artes illiberales* when I got to college. Although the Rule of St. Benedict, the founder of the order, emphasizes the importance of living by the work of one's hands, the Priory curriculum in my day didn't include a lot of training in skills that were marketable to most employers.

We did, however, learn the history of the English Benedictines who had made their way to St. Louis. Five hundred years ago, they owned and occupied Westminster Abbey in London until, as one of my teachers said, "Henry VIII pinched it from us." They briefly regained control over the abbey under the Catholic Queen Mary Tudor (a.k.a. Bloody Mary) before being ousted by her half-sister, Queen Elizabeth I. The English monks then decamped to France and settled near Nancy, where the congregation stayed until 1792, when they fled the violence of the French Revolution. At this point, they moved to Yorkshire, in the north of England, and established

Ampleforth College. The monks who founded Priory School came from Ampleforth to St. Louis in 1955.

Something the monks never mentioned, in all their many tellings of this glorious story, was the tremendous importance of beer in the history of the Benedictines. When the French booted the Benedictines out of northeast France in 1792, they didn't just get rid of a bunch of future schoolmasters. They also drove out some of the most accomplished brewers in Europe, most of whom wound up in Belgium, where they have greatly enhanced the quality of life for more than two centuries.

For more than a thousand years, Benedictine monasteries have been centers of learning, places for studying both the *artes triviales* and the *artes quadriviales*. They have also been ever mindful of the requirement imposed by Chapter 48 of *Sancti Benedicti Regula Monachorum* (The Rule of St. Benedict) to find some work for themselves. In many instances, the monasteries chose brewing. As a result, monks who followed the Rule were the first brewing scientists in Europe and developed some of the best beer styles in the world.

Today, sadly, many American beer drinkers are completely unaware of the rich variety in the spectrum of beers. Some are totally incredulous when I explain that there is more variety among beers than there is among wines. For them, the parameters are defined by the relatively small differences that distinguish the various light lagers that account for nearly all of the American market. I often point out that these light lagers differ from each other about as much as various kinds of Chablis might differ from each other. As great as the differences are that exist among Chardonnays, Cabernets, Champagnes, Ports and Sauternes, the differences among various styles of beer are probably even greater.

In order to understand the differences among styles of beer, it's worth taking a step back to consider what beer is and what distinguishes beer from wine. While wine is produced through the fermentation of fruit juice (usually, but not always, grape juice), beer is produced through the fermentation of grain extracts (usually, but not always, derived from barley). Fermentation occurs when yeast interacts with the sugars in the grain or the fruit and converts them into alcohol.

In other words, making wine involves squeezing juice from some kind of fruit and adding yeast to produce alcohol. The variations among wines are largely defined by the variations among the different grapes used in production. Brewing beer, on the other hand, first involves soaking some kind of grain extract (typically malted barley) long enough to dissolve the sugars in hot water. The resulting mixture is then allowed to cool, at which point yeast is added to produce alcohol. Many of the variations among beers are produced by varying the amounts and proportions of the different malts added to the hot water.

Typically, the fluid that is fermented to make wine is pretty much determined by the juice that comes out of the grape, with agriculture accounting for a lot of the differences among various wines. With beer, however, the fluid that is fermented is produced according to recipes and is less dependent on the whims of Mother Nature. Not only are countless varieties of grains used to brew beer, but they are prepared in myriad ways and combined in vastly different amounts and proportions.

Consider first the color of beer. Contrary to one popular misconception, the color of a beer is wholly unrelated to its alcoholic content. Some beers are opaque, yet contain relatively low amounts of alcohol; and some are almost transparent, yet pack quite a wallop. The color of a beer is simply the result of how its component malts were kilned, or cooked. Just as some coffee is roasted to produce beans that are dark and burnt, some malts are kilned differently to produce progressively darker hues, known as caramel malt, chocolate malt and black malt, among others. How these malts are blended determines the color of the beer and much of its flavor.

In general, using greater amounts of malt in any batch of beer will increase the alcoholic content of the brew. One hundred pounds of malt contain twice the amount of sugars as 50 pounds of the same malt, meaning potentially twice as much alcohol when added to the same volume of water. If you want to brew a beer with a higher alcoholic content, simply add more malt, thereby giving the yeast more sugars to convert to alcohol.

Not all malt sugars, however, are converted into alcohol. With some styles of beer, stouts for example, much of the flavor comes from these so-called "unfermented sugars." People commonly mistake the pronounced flavor of some Irish stouts for "strength" and attribute it to the presumed high level of alcohol. Similarly, some popular American lagers have low levels of unfermented sugars and correspondingly less pronounced taste, which is often mistaken for a relatively low alcoholic content.

One of the biggest variables in the flavor of beer is hops, which act as a kind of seasoning. Without going too deeply into the botany or chemistry of hops, it's enough to know that they perform the same function as many spices, both preserving the beer and adding flavor. As with peppers, there are numerous varieties of hops, each with its distinctive flavor. And, just as adding more peppers makes a batch of chili hotter and spicier, adding more hops will increase the so-called bitterness, or hoppiness, of any given brew.

The most temperamental of all the ingredients in beer is yeast, a fungus organism that converts sugars to alcohol and produces carbon dioxide as a byproduct. The process is similar to what happens when bread is made and yeast causes it to rise, inspiring the German description of beer as *flüssiges Brot* (liquid bread). The ancient Egyptians and Sumerians depended on wild yeast to ferment their beer and wine, without really knowing what it was in the air that produced the miraculous results. And, even today, the behavior of yeast can bedevil some of the best scientists in the world.

Different strains of yeast impart different flavors to beer. They also behave differently in other ways. So-called "top-fermenting" yeasts are used to make ales, typically at between 59 and 68 degrees Fahrenheit. So-called "bottom-fermenting" yeasts are used to make lagers, typically at between 41 and 48 degrees Fahrenheit.

In one sense, brewing beer seems deceptively simple. According to the *Reinheitsgebot*, the traditional German law governing the purity of beer, the only permissible ingredients are water, barley, hops and yeast. While most breweries brew most of their beers with these ingredients, wheat, corn, rice and other grains are sometimes used in addition. Nevertheless, the permutations that are possible with these relatively few ingredients are almost endless.

Among the 40 or so beers that Schlafly makes, the ales can range from relatively light Hefeweizen to much stronger Barley Wine or Imperial Stout. The lagers can range from a traditional Pilsner to an extra-strong Doppelbock. In choosing which styles to brew, we have made an effort to present a representative sampling of the beers of the world, without purporting to offer the entire universe.

The one style we have chosen not to brew is light lager, which is still the overwhelmingly predominant style in the United States. Quite simply, we see no point in brewing beers that the major breweries are already brewing far more cost effectively than we ever could.

Ours is perhaps an undertaking that could only have been launched by a bunch of liberal arts majors. Determinedly impractical in our undergraduate days, we opted for the liberal arts education that was espoused so eloquently by John Henry Newman in *The Idea of a University*. According to Newman in *On the Scope and Nature of University Education*, "A university is a place of instruction where universal knowledge is professed."

With our grounding in and reverence for the *artes liberales*, the *trivium* and the *quadrivium*, what we were doing was establishing a University of Beer, the kind of place where a Shropshire lad might want to matriculate.

THE LAW IS A ASS

Salus populi suprema lex esto.

The state motto of Missouri, expressing a sentiment found in the writings of Marcus Tullius Cicero, means "The good of the people shall be the highest law." According to Section 10-060 of Revised Missouri Statutes, this language is part of the official state seal and must be written beneath "Supporters on each side, a white or grizzly bear of Missouri, rampant, guardant proper."

My first question upon reading this particular statute was one that often pops into my mind, "What in the hell was the Missouri General Assembly thinking?" What do they mean, "white or grizzly bear of Missouri?" If the legislature likes grizzlies and polar bears, fine. So do I. But why would they enact a statute ordaining that these magnificent creatures are native to Missouri when they obviously aren't? Lewis and Clark didn't see their first grizzly bear until they reached North Dakota, which was still much too far south for polar bears. Black bear of Missouri? Maybe. White or grizzly bear of Missouri? Certainly not since Missouri entered the Union, if ever.

My second question goes to the substance of the motto. If the good of the people is so important, why didn't the General Assembly say so in English? Why did the legislators choose to proclaim this noble sentiment in a dead language that most of them and most of their constituents didn't understand? Did saying it in Latin make it easier to ignore?

While I don't know the answer to the first question, the answer to the second should be readily apparent. The General Assembly has always included a lot of lawyers, and lawyers like to use Latin whenever they can. It's not that we want to obscure what we're saying. On the contrary, we want to sound more erudite. When I was in law school, one of my classmates waged a one-woman campaign to have our diplomas printed in English, arguing, quite correctly, that few people, if any, could read a Latin diploma on her office wall. Her proposal met vigorous opposition from the rest of the class, virtually none of whom understood Latin. Notwithstanding the fact that neither they nor their families, who had helped to finance their legal educations, could understand a word of Cicero's language, they wanted their *Juris Doctor* degrees and they wanted their diplomas in Latin. Let the MBA students get degrees whose initials stood for something in English.

Like tens of thousands of other law school graduates in 1977, I emerged into a society in which lawyers were tremendously unpopular and doctors were highly revered. While, theoretically, the two so-called "learned professions" should inspire mutual respect among their members, such has not always been the case. More than once I have been subjected to anti-lawyer diatribes by doctors. On such occasions, I like to point out that while we, i.e., attorneys, were drafting the U. S. Constitution, they, i.e., physicians, were literally bleeding their patients and sticking leeches on them. So far this argument has not succeeded in winning any doctors over to my side.

In 1991, however, everything seemed to change overnight. No longer was I merely one of the thousands of lawyers in St. Louis. I was about to open the second brewery in a town that loved beer. Instead of constantly hearing the same endless complaints about lawyers or the same tiresome jokes, I now encountered gratitude and admiration in some circles. Lawyers were seen as a societal menace. By opening a brewery, I was performing a great community service. Instead of being Jesse James or Al Capone, I was suddenly Mother Teresa.

As much fun as it was to be able to take on a public persona other than that of lawyer, Charles Kopman and I have still had to call on our legal skills on numerous occasions. As I have discovered, the beer business involves a huge amount of regulation at every level of government: federal, state and local. And the fact that we were planning both to brew beer and to sell it through a retail outlet complicated the regulatory picture even more.

A big reason for the proliferation of laws and regulations is the 21st Amendment to the U. S. Constitution, which gives states and municipalities a lot more authority over alcoholic beverages than they have in other areas of interstate commerce. What creates the even bigger challenge is the reality that, however statutes and regulations might be written, their actual meaning frequently is determined by the officials in charge of administering them. As I learned time and again, it's much easier simply to accept and comply with an official's interpretation of a statute or regulation than to cite volumes of legal authority that contradict this interpretation.

The perfect illustration of this principle occurred shortly after I had incorporated the business. As I mentioned in Chapter 1, Dan and I had developed a plan for a brewpub, or a brewery attached to a restaurant. Unfortunately, brewpubs were illegal in Missouri at the time.

Following the repeal of Prohibition, Missouri, like most states, had enacted a three-tiered system of distribution for beer. In order to avoid the perceived dangers of breweries' owning and controlling taverns and thereby suppressing competition, the three levels of distribution were strictly segregated (more strictly in some states than in others). Breweries were allowed to sell only to wholesalers, which in turn were allowed to sell to retailers. Moreover, breweries were strictly forbidden to own any interest in taverns or other retailers. In other words, if we opened a brewery, we would be prohibited from holding a retail liquor license.

There was, however, an exception in the law that seemed to give us a window of opportunity. Section 311.070 of Missouri Statutes, which otherwise forbade breweries or any of their employees, officers or agents from having any kind of financial interest in a retail liquor license, did allow breweries to own a financial interest in "entertainment facilities...including, but not limited to, arenas and stadiums used primarily for concerts, shows and sporting events of all kinds."

Given our interest in the Grand Center entertainment district, this language would appear to give us the solution we had been seeking. As long as we opened our brewpub in conjunction with an entertainment facility, the prohibitions against a brewery's owning an interest in a retail establishment wouldn't be a problem. Unfortunately, the Missouri Division of Liquor Control didn't share our interpretation of the statute. When we asked the Division what kind of "entertainment facility" would meet the statutory requirements, we were told there was nothing we could open that would qualify for the exception. In essence, the phrase "including but not limited to arenas and stadiums used primarily for concerts, shows and sporting events of all kinds" in fact meant "including and absolutely limited to Busch Stadium and the Anheuser-Busch Soccer Park."

At the same time that we were exploring the possibilities for entertainment facilities that might qualify under existing Missouri law, several home-brewing enthusiasts, including Dave Miller, succeeded in persuading the General Assembly to pass a "microbrewery" law in the Spring of 1990. The bill, which became Section 311.195 of Missouri Statutes, allowed breweries holding such licenses to brew a maximum of 2,500 barrels per year (a barrel being 31 gallons, or the equivalent of 13.77 cases of

12-ounce bottles) and to hold a retail liquor license. Microbreweries were not allowed to sell beer anywhere except on their own premises. The year after this bill became law, The Saint Louis Brewery, Inc., was issued the first microbrewery license in Missouri.

On July 27, 1991, five months prior to our grand opening, the number of lawyers involved with Schlafly Beer increased by 50 percent when Dan Kopman married Sheena Cook at a church near her family's home in Aberdeenshire, Scotland. Upon moving to St. Louis, Sheena began looking for work in her specialty, which was trademark law. I referred her to a friend in the legal department at Ralston Purina, where, by chance, a trademark lawyer named Nancy Gardner was about to go on maternity leave. Sheena, who would need to go on maternity leave herself after Nancy's baby was born, was the ideal interim employee.

When Nancy came back to work at Ralston, Sheena's maternity leave took her farther than any of us expected when she went back to Scotland in the spring of 1992, and Dan followed soon thereafter. Proving that the beer gods were smiling on us once again, Nancy's husband, Ed Gordon, was available to take Dan's place, which he did for the next five years.

Ed, who had majored in business as an undergraduate at Washington University and had earned an MBA from Indiana University, brought a very different set of skills from those possessed by the liberal arts majors in whose midst he found himself. My guess is that it never would have occurred to Ed to become involved with a microbrewery if his wife hadn't bumped into Sheena through total serendipity. As it was, the coincidence was fortuitous for all concerned.

Dan, meanwhile, was back at the University of Edinburgh, earning his M.Sc. in Government Policy Studies, a degree that had absolutely nothing to do with running a brewery. He then went to work as a policy advisor and business manager for the Scottish National Blood Transfusion Service in Inverness, where his colleagues gave him the moniker "Captain Chaos."

Back in St. Louis, The Tap Room was doing well. Primarily through word of mouth, people were discovering Schlafly Beer and liking it. More and more, we were hearing from customers who loved the beer and wondered where else they could find it. The answer always surprised them,

"Nowhere else but here." "Why is that?" "Because Missouri law won't allow us to sell anywhere else." Upon hearing this news, one disappointed customer who obviously was familiar with *Oliver Twist*, by Charles Dickens, (undoubtedly another liberal arts major) exclaimed indignantly, "The law is a ass, a idiot."

We heard this kind of response often enough to convince us that we ought to try to change the law. In the fall of 1992, I began meeting with a bi-partisan group of three state senators (Democrats Wayne Goode and John Schneider and Republican Franc Flotron), who were all sympathetic. With their help, I drafted an amendment to the Missouri microbrewery law that would have raised the annual production limit for microbreweries from 2,500 barrels to 60,000 (which corresponded to the federal definition of small breweries for excise tax purposes) and would allow microbreweries to sell beer not just on their own premises, but also to licensed wholesalers.

In January of 1993, when the General Assembly convened, one of the highest priorities on Anheuser-Busch's legislative agenda was a bill that would allow grocery and convenience stores to sell beer on Sunday, which they were not then permitted to do. When Senator John Scott introduced the Sunday sales bill on behalf of Anheuser-Busch, Senator Goode, with Senators Flotron and Schneider as co-sponsors, attached our bill as an amendment. His strategy was to prevent our bill from languishing in an obscure committee somewhere, which would definitely not be the fate of A-B's Sunday sales bill.

At this point, the news media developed a keen interest in the story. My picture appeared in color on the front page of the *St. Louis Post-Dispatch* with the headline, "Tiny Brewery May Come Up Against A-B." When Anheuser-Busch lobbyist John Britton denounced our amendment, saying, "60,000 barrels, that's an inordinate amount of beer" (this from someone whose client was then producing close to 87 million barrels per year, nearly 150,000 percent of the amount he called "inordinate"), the *St. Louis Business Journal* ran the headline, "Busch lobbyist Britton helps dilute brew pub bill."

The dilution to which the *Business Journal* referred was Senator Scott's subsequent amendment to our amendment, lowering the annual production limit for microbreweries to 10,000 barrels, but allowing us to sell beer to other accounts through licensed wholesalers. The same story quotes Senator Goode as saying he advised me to talk to representatives from Anheuser-Busch to negotiate a mutually agreeable production limit.

Following this advice, I had numerous discussions with Mark Boranyak, who handled state government affairs for A-B. He eventually gave me his commitment that Anheuser-Busch would not oppose a production ceiling of 17,500 barrels per year for microbreweries. I relayed this information to Senator Goode, who added an amendment to A-B's Sunday sales bill reflecting the deal we had reached. I wasn't happy about having this legislative cap on how much beer we were allowed to brew, but I figured the bill in this form was the best I could expect this legislative session.

What happened next drew the attention of the *Wall Street Journal* on May 14, 1993, in a story with the headline, "Battling a Goliath Remains as Daunting a Task as Ever." For reasons that no one could explain, the bill with the 17,500-barrel production limit was rewritten behind closed doors, with every other provision remaining intact but with the production limit lowered to 10,000 barrels. Anheuser-Busch, which had micromanaged every other detail of the legislation, claimed to be totally unaware of how the language was changed. According to the *Journal*, "In a statement yesterday, Stephen K. Lambright, a vice president and group executive of Anheuser-Busch, said his company didn't oppose the 17,500 barrel figure. 'However, some legislators felt the increase to 17,500 barrels was too big.'"

No member of the General Assembly to whom I spoke, including the three co-sponsors of our bill, had any idea who the "some legislators" who allegedly felt this way on their own could possibly be. Nor, in all fairness, did Mark Boranyak, who had given me his personal commitment and seemed genuinely surprised that the bill had been rewritten without his realizing it.

Disappointed though we were, we moved ahead with plans to get our draft beer out into the market. The first three establishments that offered Schlafly were Blueberry Hill, in the University City Loop, Cardwell's in Clayton, and the Trainwreck in Brentwood. I still remember my exhilaration on the evening in August of 1993 when, for the first time, I was able to walk up to the bar somewhere other than at The Tap Room and order a Schlafly. It's also interesting that I was able to call on all of our retail accounts in less than an hour.

Before too long, customers began asking for bottled Schlafly. Some restaurants weren't equipped to offer our draft beer. And, more important, approximately 80 percent of the beer in the United States is sold in so-called "off-premise" locations, such as supermarkets and convenience stores. Until we offered packaged beer, we were going to miss out on this important part of the market.

There was, however, the legislatively imposed annual production limit. It simply didn't make economic sense to add a bottling line if we weren't able to brew more than 10,000 barrels per year. We therefore began to look for a contract brewer, a brewery that would brew and bottle Schlafly Beer according to our specifications. We finally struck a deal with August Schell in New Ulm, Minnesota, and introduced bottled Schlafly into the St. Louis market in June of 1996.

Once again, the reception we got was very gratifying, so much so that we soon concluded that there really was enough demand for bottled Schlafly to justify putting in our own bottling line, provided that the State of Missouri allowed us to brew enough beer to meet this demand. In 1997 I went back to the General Assembly with another bill to raise the production limit for microbreweries and found out that the climate had changed.

No longer was there any organized opposition to our brewing more beer. I learned that I didn't have to change the microbrewery law. All we had to do was apply for a different type of license, a so-called "22 Percent License." This was similar to what wineries were issued and would permit us to produce unlimited amounts of fermented alcoholic beverages, as long as they had an alcoholic content below 22 percent, which was far higher than that of any beer we were capable of brewing or would want to brew.

With this licensing matter resolved, two other transitions occurred in 1997, which was also the year that Schlafly was sold in Busch Stadium for the first time. First, Dan and Sheena moved back to St. Louis. Second, Ed and Nancy moved to Atlanta, which was closer to his family in Florida. Dan resumed the role of full-time chief operating officer; and Ed's role evolved into one of advising on some of the trickier accounting and financial matters.

Apart from the licensing, opening a new brewery with its own bottling line was still a major step, far bigger than any we had contemplated since opening in 1991. Since that time, most of our expansion had been incremental. We had gradually added more fermentation tanks to our brewery on Locust Street. We had gradually expanded the kitchen. We had gradually renovated additional space in the current building. And we had gradually expanded our workforce. What we were now contemplating was a much bigger brewery in a much more expensive building.

After finding some very good used equipment at affordable prices, we set out to find a location for the new brewery. Having reached the capacity of our brewery on Locust Street, we wanted a new facility that would be capable of producing 25,000 to 35,000 barrels per year, depending on the mix of ales and lagers. While we looked at dozens and dozens of potential sites, we concentrated our search on former supermarkets for a couple of reasons. First, they had enough square footage on the ground floor to accommodate a brewery and packaging line, along with good loading dock access. Second, unlike a lot of industrial buildings, they tended to be located near where people lived, thereby providing better locations for a restaurant.

We finally chose a former Shop 'N Save store at 7260 Southwest Avenue in Maplewood, an inner-ring suburb adjoining the City of St. Louis. The building, which had previously housed a Kroger store, had been vacant for eight years when we bought it in September of 2001, shortly after 9/11. Because of its location at the eastern edge of town, both the Maplewood Chamber of Commerce and the City of Maplewood (a client of my law firm) were very eager for us to move in and start generating street life near that portion of Manchester Road, the city's main commercial thoroughfare. It was perhaps in response to this community pressure that Citizens National Bank, with headquarters almost directly across the street, provided us with financing at rates much more favorable than those offered by any other bank.

With a project much greater in scope than the renovation of the Swift Building, and far more expensive, construction and installation of equipment took longer than we anticipated. We finally celebrated the grand opening of Schlafly Bottleworks on April 7, 2003, the 70th anniversary of one of the most important dates in brewing history. While the 21st Amendment wasn't ratified until December 5, 1933, thereby repealing the

18th Amendment and expunging Prohibition from the U. S. Constitution, legislation that took effect on April 7, 1933, legalized beer with an alcoholic content up to 3.2 percent by weight (4.0 percent by volume).

This law, which we have celebrated in three subsequent "Repeal Festivals," is perhaps nearer and dearer to the hearts of beer drinkers than any law since the *Reinheitsgebot*, the beer purity law proclaimed by Duke Wilhelm IV of Bavaria in 1516, which at the time limited the ingredients allowed in beer to barley, hops and water. What many beer drinkers, especially beer chauvinists from Germany, might not realize, however, is that in 1268, two and a half centuries earlier, King Louis IX of France had issued what amounted to an extensive consumer protection law for beer drinkers, one provision of which prescribed that "Nothing shall enter the composition of beer, but good malt and hops."

How fitting that such a law should be decreed by a king who would later be canonized and become the patron saint of a city renowned throughout the world for its beer. At least with respect to beer drinkers, King Louis truly was a ruler for whom *salus populi* was the *suprema lex*.

DEMOCRACY AND CUCKOO CLOCKS

In Italy for 30 years under the Borgias they had warfare, terror, murder, bloodshed—they produced Michelangelo, Leonardo da Vinci and the Renaissance. In Switzerland they had brotherly love, 500 years of democracy and peace, and what did they produce? The cuckoo clock.

Being of Swiss descent, I have to take issue with this characterization of my ancestral homeland by Harry Lime, who was played by Orson Welles in *The Third Man*. Despite the popular misconception perpetuated by Mark Twain, among others, the cuckoo clock was, in fact, not invented in Switzerland, but rather in the German *Schwarzwald* (Black Forest) in 1738.

Switzerland was, however, where August Schlafly was born on May 4, 1850, in the village of Steinhof, Canton Solothurn, roughly midway between Basel and Bern. In 1854 his family emigrated to the United States and landed in New Orleans. They headed up the Mississippi River and settled in the town of New Helvetia (now Highland), Illinois. Shortly after their arrival, John Joseph Schlafly, August's father, died of cholera, leaving his widow, Helena, with five young children and pregnant with a sixth, August's sister Emma.

After her husband's death, Helena moved to the nearby town of Carlyle, where she supported her six young children by taking in laundry. Adding to the challenges faced by the immigrant family was the rise of the Know-Nothing Party, a nativist movement based on prejudice against Catholics and immigrants, among others. According to Schlafly family lore, the Know-Nothings prevented August and his siblings from attending the public elementary school in Carlyle.

The same family lore includes a Jewish neighbor who tutored the Schlafly children, providing my great-grandfather with the only formal education he ever received (with the possible exception of a short stint in school before the Know-Nothings drove him out). Whether the story, as passed down through the generations, is 100 percent true or not, August's children and grandchildren all agreed that he was immensely grateful to the unnamed Jewish gentleman in Carlyle.

Despite his limited education, August Schlafly was an energetic entrepreneur who became involved in businesses as varied as banking, lumber and bottled spring water. Upon his death, he left different businesses to each of his sons, with my grandfather, Fred Schlafly, becoming president of Mountain Valley Water Company, whose spring was in Hot Springs, Arkansas, with headquarters in St. Louis. My father, Daniel Schlafly, later succeeded his father as president of Mountain Valley. Along the way, they had acquired the Pepsi-Cola bottling franchise in Little Rock, which they operated as the Arkansas Beverage Company.

Although the family interests in Mountain Valley and the Pepsi-Cola bottling operation had been sold long before I became interested in starting a brewery, I like to say that the Schlaflys have been swimming upstream in the beverage business for more than a century. First, we bought a business that marketed expensive bottled water in an economically challenged state like Arkansas, where Yankees from St. Louis weren't particularly welcome (so unwelcome, in fact, that the Ku Klux Klan once burned a cross on my great-grandfather's lawn, presumably because he was a foreign-born Catholic). Then we started bottling and selling Pepsi-Cola in the heart of the South, where Coca-Cola reigned supreme. The only venture that could possibly be more foolish would be opening a brewery in the shadow of Anheuser-Busch. It must be the stubbornness in those Swiss genes that makes us do such things.

Shortly after the turn of the 20th century, August Schlafly moved from Carlyle to St. Louis, along with his wife and family. It was in St. Louis that his son Fred met and married my grandmother, Eleanor Lyons, who was proudly Irish and unashamedly anti-German. Although she loved my grandfather dearly, she had great misgivings about the fact that the name Schlafly, which she had assumed upon marrying into the family, sounded German.

I remember once visiting my grandparents, along with several cousins, and hearing one of my grandmother's customary discourses on the superiority of Irish culture, especially with respect to Germans. As we sat in rapt attention, my grandfather was on the other side of the room reading the newspaper. He appeared not to be hearing anything until my grandmother got to the topic of music, where, once again, she explained to us how magnificent the Irish were, particularly in comparison with the oafish Germans. Granddad lowered his paper and asked, "Excuse me, Ella. I forget. How many symphonies came out of Ireland?" He then resumed reading the paper, leaving my grandmother to explain that we had just seen a typical display of German rudeness.

Considering that my ancestry is roughly one-eighth Swiss and seven-eighths Irish, I often say that my Irish genes got me interested in beer, and my Swiss genes are responsible for wanting to translate this interest into a business. Whenever I make this observation, Dan Kopman is always quick to add that I needed a Jewish partner to make the business successful. I can't disagree.

Actually, my Irish ancestry is a little more muddled. On both my father's and my mother's sides, my ancestors include almost equal numbers of Catholic and Protestant Irish. On my father's side, the Catholic Lyonses and Burkes came to St. Louis directly from Ireland, while the Protestant Allens went from Ulster to Eastern Tennessee to Southern Illinois, where Jane Allen met and married August Schlafly. On the maternal side, the Catholic McBrides went from Western New York State, where they worked on the Erie Canal, to Western Pennsylvania, where my great-grandfather William McBride started out in the oil business and where my mother's mother Laura McBride Mahaffey was born, to St. Louis, where my great-grandfather relocated his business in 1908. On my mother's paternal side, one of my Protestant Mahaffey forebears came as an indentured servant in the early 18th century to Delaware, from where his descendants made their way south to the Carolinas, then west through Appalachia and then to Hopkins County, Texas, where my grandfather Birch Oliver Mahaffey was born. Birch Mahaffey left Texas to go to West Point; was expelled from West Point but was nevertheless commissioned as an officer in the U. S. Army; married Laura McBride and moved with her to Hawaii, where he was stationed when my mother's older sister was born; then left the Army and moved to St. Louis, where the couple was living when my mother, Adelaide Mahaffey Schlafly, was born on July 19, 1915.

The upshot is that I consider myself a metaphor for St. Louis. My four grandparents were born in four different states (Illinois, Missouri, Pennsylvania and Texas), but had all settled in St. Louis prior to the U. S. entry into the First World War. Just as the world converged on St. Louis around the time of the World's Fair of 1904, so did my family. Now, one century later, I'm still living in the same neighborhood (Central West End) where all four of my grandparents and six of my great-grandparents lived. Ulrike and I live across the street from the house where my mother grew up and directly behind the house where I grew up. If, as some people say, St. Louis has a high regard for tradition, no one is more traditional than I am, at least when it comes to choice of residence.

I would be the first to say that I was fortunate to grow up in very comfortable circumstances. I never had to contend with the economic des-

peration that surely confronted the Schlafly family in Carlyle, where an un-
educated immigrant mother who spoke little or no English had to support
six children without any help from their deceased father. Nor was my situation like that of the young William McBride, who never finished elementary
school because he went to work as a Western Union delivery boy in the oil-
fields of Western Pennsylvania in order to support his family. Nor did I have
to worry about the poverty of East Texas, which Birch Mahaffey escaped
through an appointment to West Point, affording him an education that he
could never have hoped to get otherwise.

I was brought up well aware of the advantages I possessed and equal-
ly aware of the obligations they entailed. Both of my parents constantly
stressed the value of service to others. This was a lesson taught not only
with words, but mainly by example. While they were supportive of all kinds
of charities and causes, my mother and father concentrated most of their
efforts on social justice and education.

My mother was very active for a long time in the Missouri Association for Social Welfare, an advocacy group for the disadvantaged. Years
before the federal Civil Rights Act of 1964, she was traveling to Jefferson
City, the state capital, to lobby for legislation that would prohibit places of
public accommodation (e.g., hotels and restaurants) from discriminating on
the basis of race.

My father served on the St. Louis Board of Education from 1953 to
1981. He was initially elected as a reformer to help clean up the corruption
that was particularly rampant in the schools' building department. Shortly
after his election, the school board faced the challenge of dismantling the
segregated system that was mandated by the Missouri Constitution. My father soon became a strong advocate for integration and pursued this cause
long after leaving the board.

In 1967, he became the Chairman of the Board of Trustees at St.
Louis University, a Jesuit institution, thereby becoming the first lay person to chair the governing board of a major Catholic college in the United
States. This was a time of turmoil on campuses all across America; yet I have
heard consistent praise for his leadership from the students with whom he
dealt, all of whom are around my age. In 1979, the University awarded him
its Fleur-de-Lis Medal, which was then its highest award. In the same year,
Universitas, the SLU alumni magazine, wrote that he was the University's
"Man of the Decade." Ten years later, St. Louis University recognized the

accomplishments of both my mother and my father by awarding them honorary degrees.

Broadly speaking, the organizations and causes to which I myself have devoted my time and money over the years fall into two categories. First would be those from which I personally have benefited. As a beneficiary of the services provided, I feel an obligation to give back in some way. An obvious example would be KWMU, a local public radio station. As a regular listener, I ought to help pay for the programming. I also do monthly commentaries on the station and participate in the on-air solicitations for donations.

In this vein of giving back, I have been supportive of the schools where I was educated. Recognizing that my education was subsidized by donors who had gone before me, and that not even full tuition covered the total cost of this education, I have felt that the only way to repay the earlier benefactors of my education is to assist future generations. To that end, I have served on both the Georgetown University Board of Regents and the Priory School Board of Advisors, and have contributed to the alumni funds of both institutions.

The second category of charities would be those that help people much less fortunate than I am for one reason or another. For example, I co-chaired "Dining Out For Life," a program through which St. Louis restaurants raise money for people with AIDS, though I derive no direct, personal gain from the program. Likewise, I serve on the board of a hospital in Milot, Haiti, not because I am ever going to need the services it offers, but rather because the patients desperately need help from those of us who are lucky enough to live in more prosperous societies. It was in this spirit that Ulrike and I spent a week in April of 2006 in New Orleans, rebuilding a home that was severely damaged by Hurricane Katrina.

The cause to which I have probably devoted the most time over the years is the St. Louis Public Library. Like a lot of things in life, my initial involvement was totally serendipitous. In 1984 I received a call from the office of St. Louis Mayor Vincent Schoemehl, inquiring whether I'd be interested in serving on the Library Board. I had never heard of it. I ended up being appointed to the Board of Directors of the Public Library by Mayor Schoemehl and re-appointed by the three mayors who succeeded him.

The library combines elements of both types of charities. Having received my first library card in 1957, I am a patron who continues to take advantage of library services. But the library also has extensive programs to benefit the sizeable disadvantaged population of St. Louis, one example being that it offers computer access to people who cannot afford to purchase their own computers.

Serving on the Library Board has been rewarding on a number of levels. The operation is small enough that what I do can make a noticeable difference and large enough to have an impact on the community. It also meets the criteria of both types of charities I tend to support. I see my involvement both as repaying my personal debt for what the library has done for me and as benefiting the less fortunate who depend on its services.

At this point, it would be perfectly reasonable to ask, "What does all this talk about charities have to do with opening a brewery? Surely you're not suggesting that brewing and selling beer is your idea of serving mankind?" Quite right. We did not start the brewery with the intention of doing anything eleemosynary. Nevertheless, it's fair to say that we did a lot more good for the community than we ever would have imagined at the outset.

When we opened on Locust Street in 1991, we had rehabilitated a building that had been vacant for 22 years. We provided new jobs and contributed to the revitalization of the neighborhood. Nearby lofts with 900 square feet are now selling for more than we paid for a 40,000-square foot building and adjoining parking lot in 1991. Most observers would agree that the presence of The Tap Room has been a major factor in the revival.

When we opened Bottleworks in Maplewood in 2003, we had rehabilitated a building that had been vacant since 1993. Our presence encouraged other businesses to locate near us and helped to revive the eastern end of Manchester Road. We added more jobs, bringing the total on our payroll to approximately 180 at any given time.

I vividly recall our grand opening in Maplewood on April 7, 2003. Hundreds, perhaps even thousands, of people were attracted out of curiosity or by the lure of free beer. Nearby traffic was extremely congested and crowds were spilling out of our parking lot. Amidst the chaos, an older gentleman approached me and asked, "Are you Mr. Shaffley?" (This wasn't the first or last time my last name has been mispronounced.) When I said I was, he continued, "Well, I live just down the street here, lived there for 40 years."

I cringed. I was positive that someone had parked in front of his driveway, or someone had littered on his lawn, or somehow we had managed to inconvenience him. Instead, he said something that astonished me: "I just want to thank you for what you've done. I've lived here a long time and it seems like a lot of people have forgotten about us in this neighborhood. I can't thank you enough for bringing some life back into it." While I certainly didn't get into the beer business with any pretensions of saving the world, this moment confirmed my realization that we really were making a positive contribution to the community.

Prior to our opening in 1991, when I talked to my parents about the venture, their reaction was definitely not that I was embarking on a noble project that would uplift the community. On the contrary, they, like many other observers, thought it was the stupidest thing they had ever heard of. My father pointed out that dozens of breweries had gone broke trying to compete with Anheuser-Busch in St. Louis; that the building we had chosen was in an awful state of disrepair; that the neighborhood had been abandoned; that the restaurant business was extremely risky; and, incidentally, that I knew nothing about running a brewery, operating a restaurant or being in the real estate business. He was absolutely right.

One of the constant bits of advice I heard from my parents between 1989, when I incorporated the business, and 1991, when we officially opened, was to limit my losses. On numerous occasions, my father encouraged me to set a limit on the investment I was willing to lose and to have the discipline to stick with it. If my losses exceeded this figure, I needed to be prepared not to throw more good money after bad. I think their concern was not simply that I was embarking on a risky venture and could lose a lot of money, but I was doing so in St. Louis, where everybody would know how foolish I had been. It would be one thing to lose money on a dumb investment out of town. But to do so locally, in the media spotlight, with hundreds of thousands of skeptics prepared to say "I told you so," would have the additional disadvantage for them of public embarrassment because of their foolhardy son.

Despite their misgivings, my parents came to our grand opening. Nine months later, we had a big party at The Tap Room for my father's 80th birthday, which was September 29, 1992. At the end of the evening he put his arm around me and said, "Tom, this is really marvelous. I want to invest in it." Suddenly the idea of opening a brewery wasn't so cuckoo after all.

WHAT'S IN A NAME?

What's in a name? That which we call a rose
By any other name would smell as sweet.

Juliet's famous query in Shakespeare's *Romeo and Juliet* brings to mind the myriad aspects of what is today called "branding." Brewing good beer was a *sine qua non*, but it was just the start. A crucial step in figuring out how to market the beer was deciding what to call it. While the Book of Genesis tells us that Adam named all the beasts of the earth on the sixth day of creation, it took Dan Kopman and me a whole lot longer to come up with a name for the beer we were planning to brew.

When we incorporated in 1989, we called our company The Saint Louis Brewery, Inc. simply in order to have a name to put on the incorporation papers filed with the Missouri Secretary of State. The name described what we planned to do and where we planned to do it. And we thought the definite article "The" conferred distinctiveness on our enterprise. We figured there was plenty of time to decide later what we would actually call the beer.

As our long-anticipated opening approached, the need to name the beer became more urgent. There's almost no category of name we didn't consider. We talked about historical figures associated with St. Louis (Louis IX, Pierre Laclede, Lewis & Clark, Daniel Boone, Mark Twain, Jesse James, Charles Lindbergh). We thought of all kinds of animals, some indigenous to the region, some not (Bullfrog, Catfish, Gray Squirrel, Channel Cat, Bobcat, Bison). We considered the names of Native American tribes (Osage, Cherokee, Chippewa); various types of vehicles (Steamboat, Paddlewheel, Locomotive, Caboose); different types of trees (Sycamore, Pin Oak, Chestnut) and even a type of stone (Limestone, in recognition of the limestone caves historically used to store beer beneath the City of St. Louis). We also talked about humorous names and plays on words (Brew Ha Ha).

After considering these and hundreds of other names in dozens of categories, we needed to narrow our focus. First, Dan emphasized that we didn't want to make fun of our beer or invite others to do so. While a catfish may seem colorful and figures prominently in local lore, we really didn't want people to associate our beer with a scavenger at the bottom of a polluted river. Second, Dan also pointed out that hundreds of breweries over the years have borne the family names of their founders. Putting one's name on the beer sends the message that the founder personally vouches

August and Jane Allen Schlafly on their 50th wedding anniversary, 1924. Tom's father, Dan, is the boy on the left closest to the front.

August Schlafly (1850-1934).

Daniel Lyons Schlafly, Tom's father, 1983.

Adelaide Mahaffey Schlafly, Tom's mother, 1934.

Samuel L. Sherer, the architect who designed 2100
Locust Street, standing in front of the St. Louis Art
Museum, where he served as Director in the 1920s.

Downtown firestorm, 1976.(Photo by Lt. Donald E. Strate, Retired, St. Louis Metropolitan Police Dept.)

2100 Locust Street, which was vacant from 1969 to 1991, when it became the home of Schlafly Beer.

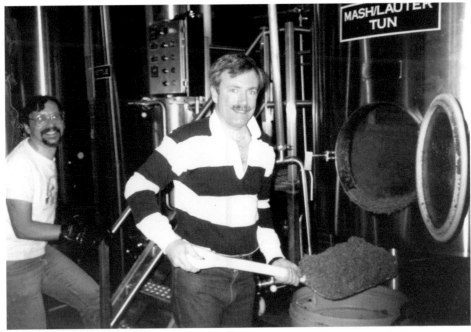

Tom assisting with brewing under the watchful eye of Dave Miller, 1992.

Tom Flood during his first stint at the Tap Room, 1992.

The sign that inadvertently gave our first restaurant its name.

Ed Gordon, Chief Financial Officer.

Charles Kopman, member of the board of directors of The Saint Louis Brewery, Inc.

Dan Kopman and Tom Schlafly on the brewing platform at the opening of The Tap Room, 1991.

Sara and Stephen Hale. (Photograph by David Torrence, who was influenced by Grant Wood)

Finnish beer connoisseur Mark Naski, loyal customer from the beginning.

The Schlafly Oktoberfest Run, 1994.

Tom at finish line of New York marathon, 1994.

Samoan strongman Vae Mafuli pulling the Schlafly truck at the Microfest beer festival, 2000.
Sparky and Koko (1999-2002), two Chesapeake Retrievers, are looking on with their owner.

Daniel Schlafly in a photograph accompanying an article in the Oct. 3, 1960 issue of Time magazine on School Board reform in St. Louis (Art Fillmore, Time magazine).

Ulrike and Tom at a primary school in Haiti, 2005.

In New Orleans, helping to rebuild a home damaged by Hurricane Katrina, 2005.

The Courthouse Steps, the singing lawyers for whom Tom writes lyrics.

German artist Karin Kneffel's painting of hops, commissioned by Tom and Ulrike.

Mystery Solved, Variously
By JimWallace

The column (*SPELL/Binder*, March/April 1994) about the untitled alliterative poem discovered in an 1891 almanac elicited a number of interesting responses. Several SPELL members even studied versions of the poem in school, and two readers had family ties to the mysterious city, Yassy, cited in the penultimate line.

The most interesting authorship theory, probably apocryphal, comes from **Tom Schlafly**, of St. Louis. The story goes that the poem, which he memorized in English class 30 years ago, was written by a class at Eton, with a different classmate writing each line. "In any case," Mr. Schlafly writes, "this memory inspired me to try to duplicate the feat for a local poetry contest earlier this year."

Here's the Schlafly version. Maybe it will appear in an almanac some day.

HEADLINES

Arafat and Aristide and aliens appear,
Bracketed by Bigfoot, Bobbitt-bashing, beer.
Christophe's cutting Chelsea, Clinton's critics cry.
Donahue dares doubters: Demjanjuk's dating Di.
Endomorphic Elvis envied E.T.'s ears.
Fergie's fighting fat. Farrakhan fuels fears.
Generally good grades grudgingly given GATT.
Hillary's hyping healthcare. Headlines hype her hat.
Inman is incongruous. Intelligence issue irks.
Jesse Jackson jabs jivin' juvenile jerks.
KKK killed Kennedy. Kwashiorkor killed Khartoum.
Leno's lady leaving; Lesbian lovers loom.
Marla Maples Marries. Marla's masochistic
Needs now nurtured nicely: Nurturer's narcissistic.
Ounces off. Ounces on. Oprah's overweight.
Priestly pederasty puzzles pontiff's pate.
Quayle's quizzing quells Quixotic quota queen.
Robber-rapist rap, Rushdie rock Racine.
Sources scorn *Spectator*'s sordid story: State
Troopers tell tall tales that try to titillate.
UFOs unlikely. Universities uproarious.
Varicose veins vanquished. Valium victorious.
Worldly Wellesley women want, when woefully wan,
Xavier, X, Xanthippe, Xerxes, Xenophon,
Yahweh, Yevtushenko, Yeltsin, Yucatanistas,
Zorro, Zoroaster, Zappa, Zapatistas.

From the July/August 1994 issue of SPELL/Binder, the newsletter of the Society for the Preservation of English Language and Literature.

Crest logo created in 1991.

Logo, created for the bottle labels in 1996.

"Brewed in Saint Louis" logo as revised for the opening of Schlafly Bottleworks in 2003, to reflect that the bottled beer was now being brewed in St. Louis.

Tom and Ulrike celebrating their engagement with Tom's mother and Trudy Busch at Grant's Farm, 1995.

Wedding in St. Louis, September 2, 1995.

Flower girl Christina Valentine (Gussie Busch's granddaughter) and junior bridesmaid Margaret Shafer (Tom's niece). (Photo by Josephine Havlak)

In Cologne with Heinrich Becker, Managing Partner of Privatbrauerei Gaffel, 1999.

In Cologne with Ulrike's uncle, Dr. Max Adenauer, son of German Chancellor Konrad Adenauer.

Heinrich Becker and Tom, prior to the Karneval Parade in Cologne, 1997.

Cologne Cathedral, June 8, 1996.

Trudy Busch hosting a party at Grant's Farm for Tom's 50th birthday.

The beer for all occasions.

A license plate honors the favorite beer in Cologne.

With CARE at Tempelhof Airport in Berlin on the 50th anniversary of The Berlin Airlift, 1998. (The jacket was borrowed from Gail Halvorsen, the famous "Candy Bomber" during The Airlift).

Selection of Schlafly Beer styles available at various times throughout the year.

James "Otto" Ottolini, 1998.

Sheena and Dan Kopman at The Tap Room on Burns Night.

Bill Dorman, Paul Jensen and Stephen Hale, Burns Night, 1996.

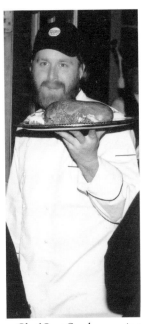

Chef Scot Smelser serving haggis on Burns Night.

Future Mayor Francis Slay with loyal patrons at The Tap Room, 1998.

Tom Schlafly

Owner
Tap Room Restaurant, Bottleworks,
Schlafly Brand Beers

When he's not practicing law at Blackwell Sanders Peper Martin, Tom Schlafly is a microbrewer and restaurateur. He opened the Tap Room, located a few blocks northwest of Union Station, in 1991 and the Bottleworks restaurant and bottling plant in Maplewood in 2003. The building is credited with jump-starting the revitalization along Maplewood's stretch of Manchester Road. Schlafly is a member of Courthouse Steps, a group of singing St. Louis attorneys that pokes fun at national and local individuals and events. He also is a regular commentator on KWMU-FM. Among his volunteer activities, he serves on the boards of Trailnet and the St. Louis Public Library Foundation.

Schlafly Beer at the St. Louis Art Fair, 1996.

Soulard Mardi Gras, early 1990s.

Pale Ale, the most popular Schlafly style.

In Budvar, Czech Republic, 2001.

Adelaide Schlafly at The Tap Room on
her 90th birthday, July 19, 2005.

BEST NEW BAR

THE TAP ROOM-
ST. LOUIS BREWERY

photo by Mike DeFilippo

Daniel L. Schlafly, Influential Civic Leader, Dies At 84

By Robert W. Duffy
Cultural News Editor of the Post-Dispatch

Daniel L. Schlafly, a man whose life was distinguished by an intuitive understanding of the concept of *noblesse oblige*, died Wednesday (July 16, 1997) of a brain tumor at his home in the Central West End. He was 84.

the most public-spirited citizens I have ever known. There aren't too many Dan Schlaflys kicking around this country anymore."

Daniel Lyons Schlafly was born to J.F. and Eleanor Lyons Schlafly in 1912. As a youngster he went to the old Barat Hall school and graduated first in his class from St. Louis Uni-

Kölsch vom Mississippi

Tom Schlafly ließ die Juristerei ruhen und verlegte sich vor zehn Jahren erfolgreich aufs Bierbrauen

St. Louis, MO - Tom Schlafly (53) muss ein mutiger Mann sein. Ein Abenteurer, ein Kämpfer. Einer, der es mit jedem Gegner aufnimmt und sich nicht in die Knie zwingen lässt. Vielleicht aber ist Schlafly auch einfach ein bisschen verrückt; besessen von seinem Beruf - im positiven Sinne.

Jedenfalls erschließt es sich nicht so leicht, warum ein erfolgreicher Rechtsanwalt und Georgetown-Absolvent von jetzt auf gleich das Fach wechselt und sich als kleiner Bierbrauer versucht. Noch dazu im Vorhof des Gerstensaft-Giganten - in St. Louis, dem Sitz des Weltmarktführers Anheuser-Busch. Schlafly indes weiß auf die Frage nach dem Grund seiner beruflichen Kursänderung eine bestechend einfache Antwort: „Ich habe mich eigentlich schon immer für Bier interessiert." Wer nicht.

Schlafly jedoch hat allen Grund zum Feiern. Zehn Jahre wird seine Firma in diesen Tagen alt. Und: Das Geschäft läuft gut. 12 000 Hektoliter Bier werden im Jahr 2001 Schlaflys Brau-Kessel verlassen. Im Gründungsjahr 1991 waren es nur 1500 Hektoliter, die zudem noch ausnahmslos im angeschlossenen Restaurant ausgeschenkt wurden.

„Das war damals der einzige Ort im Universum, wo man unser Bier bekam", sagt Schlafly mit einem Augenzwinkern. Heute sind die 35 verschiedenen Sorten in vielen Kneipen erhältlich. Und auch die Zahl der Mitarbeiter hat sich vervielfacht: Mittlerweile arbeiten 70 Angestellte in dem schmucken Altbau an der 2100 Locust Street in St. Louis.

Sein Ur-Großvater August Schlafly (1850-1934) könnte also zurecht stolz auf seinen Nachfahren sein. Der Einwanderer aus dem Schweizer Kanton Solothurn hatte nämlich schon 1907 das Getränke-Geschäft als lohnend erkannt und deshalb die Mountain Valley Quelle in Arkansas erworben. Spätere Generationen verlegten sich schließlich darauf, Pepsi-Cola abzufüllen. Aber erst mit Tom Schlafly drangen die Amerikaner Schweizer Herkunft in die Bier-Branche vor. Ein nachhaltiger Schritt, den Schlafly nie bereut

Produziert nicht für den Massengeschmack: Tom Schlafly.

hat.

Wahrscheinlich liegt das an seinem Erfolgsrezept: „Wir versuchen eine große Anzahl von Biersorten abseits des amerikanischen Massengeschmacks anzubieten. Wir brauen unter anderem Kölsch, Hefe-Weizen, Maibock und Alt", sagt der Chef und ergänzt: „Vor allem deutsche Biersorten!" Schlafly lacht. „Vom Brauen verstehen die Deutschen eben eine Menge. Gerade als Bierbrauer haben sie einen exzellenten Ruf in den USA."

Deshalb hat sich Schlafly auch Deutsch angeeignet, „Kneipendeutsch", wie er bescheiden sagt: „Das kann in diesem Gewerbe niemals schaden." Privat hat ihm die Fremdsprache jedenfalls großes Glück beschert. Seine Frau Ulrike stammt aus Köln.

„Und ausgerechnet sie war, ehe wir uns kennen lernten, eine ausgesprochen überzeugte Weintrinkerin." Tom Schlafly, der spätberufene Bierbrauer, war eben schon immer ein mutiger Mann.

Jörg Diehl

Mitch Turner, brand manager.

Tom and Stephen Hale at bottle launch party, 1996.

Mike Prokopf (right) with a former sous-chef, 1994.

Scott Le Corgne as restaurant manager, before he moved to sales.

Jack Petrovic at bottle launch party, 1996.

Kevin Nash, bartender.

Christian Artzner, beer quality manager (Photo West End Word.)

Sparky delivering the first keg of Schlafly Beer to Busch Stadium, April, 1997.

Sparky (1987-2000). (Drawing by Ann B. Wilson)

Barley (2000 -).

Bill Gates and Tom discussing their shared birthday, October 28, at the United Way Alexis de Tocqueville dinner, 1998.

German artist Markus Lüpertz at The Tap Room, 2003.

H. E. Jürgen Chrobog, German Ambassador to the United States at The Tap Room, 1996.

SUNDAY, JANUARY 3, 1999   ST. LOUIS POST-DISPATCH

Holy Smoke beer will honor pope's visit; will be ready Wednesday

If Pope John Paul II stops by the Tap Room at 2100 Locust Street during his visit to St. Louis

Francis Slay, future Mayor of St. Louis, at the opening of the north bar at The Tap Room, 1998.

Father Christopher Hanson, Saint Louis Abbey.

Rabbi Joe Rosenbloom, Temple Emmanuel.

Canon Cricket Cooper, Christ Church Cathedral.

Bottleworks employees as shown in an advertisement for the St. Louis Originals, 2006.

Hop in the City, September 15, 2001, prior to the moment of silence for 9/11 victims.

Schlafly Bottleworks, 2004. (Photograph by Alise O'Brien)

The St. Louis Post-Dispatch acknowledges the opening of Schlafly Bottleworks in Maplewood, April 19, 2003. (Drawing by Dan Martin)

ST. LOUIS POST-DISPATCH   (4)

Maplewood OKs microbrewery

for it and is willing to stake his or her reputation on its quality. The fact that Schlafly sounds German had the added benefit of linking us with the long tradition of breweries named for their German-American founders.

I'm reminded of Ronnoco Coffee Company in St. Louis, which was founded by the O'Connor family in the early 20th century. With the apparent rationale that the coffee would seem more authentic if it had a Spanish name, the brand became Ronnoco, which is O'Connor spelled backwards. Luckily for us, Schlafly sounds sufficiently German to give us an aura of authenticity without having to change my name in any way. It sounds so authentic, in fact, that I once got into a polite argument with a customer who insisted that he had seen memorabilia from the old Schlafly Brewery and who refused to believe my insistence that the brewery hadn't existed prior to 1991.

This gentleman wasn't the first or only person to make the mistaken assumption that Schlafly Beer had been around for a long time. On more than one occasion I have overheard customers at The Tap Room explain to others in their parties that we were one of the old pre-Prohibition breweries that were so prevalent in St. Louis. The fact that our building (which had been the home of a printing company) is a magnificent old brick structure, with floors and beams of old-growth Douglas fir, has undoubtedly reinforced these misrepresentations, which I have not gone out of my way to correct.

Having decided to call our beer Schlafly, we planned to call our restaurant The Saint Louis Brewery in order to underscore the fact that we were brewing our beer on the premises. "Come to The Saint Louis Brewery, the home of Schlafly Beer" was our intended message. We decided to call the downstairs restaurant "The Tap Room" to make the point that all of our beer was served from taps. And we decided to call the upstairs room "The Club Room," which would be available for private parties and where we would feature live music on weekends. So far, so good.

By December 26, 1991, the downstairs restaurant was ready to open for business, but work on the second floor was far from complete. The most visible sign on the building was for The Tap Room. Our customers took notice of the sign and began referring to the entire operation as The Tap Room, not as The Saint Louis Brewery or as the Schlafly Brewery. This was but one of many instances of our best laid plans' being foiled. We had listed Schlafly Beer and The Saint Louis Brewery in the telephone directory, but not The Tap Room. Unfortunately, a lot of our customers knew our business only by a name we had not thought to list in the phone book and not by either of the two names we had listed. I was told that some directory assistance operators got so many inquiries about The Tap Room that they learned to reply by asking callers if they wanted the number for The Saint Louis Brewery or for Schlafly Beer.

In short, to the extent that we had a plan for branding, it wasn't terribly effective. For years after we opened, I would encounter people who said they had never heard of Schlafly Beer, only to find out that they had been to The Tap Room frequently and had enjoyed our beer. Even though all the brewing was done behind glass right next to the dining room, some of our customers were able to visit The Tap Room repeatedly without realizing they were in a brewery or that there was a beer called Schlafly.

Our decision to come out with bottled beer in 1996 caused us to re-examine our approach to branding. One of the fundamental changes we made was to our logo. When we first opened, we had adopted a crest that incorporated the seal of Steinhof, the village in Switzerland where August Schlafly had been born. We took the Swiss ibex and mountains from the Steinhof seal, embellished the seal with hops and barley, and added the name Schlafly across the top. The end result was very elegant and we were all quite taken with it, at least until we met with the folks at Core, an advertising agency located in a nearby loft on Washington Avenue.

According to Core, the problem was that our seal looked too elegant. One of the owners of the agency said it sent the message that we were Americans trying to pass themselves off as Europeans. He also said that yuppies would buy products with a blue collar image, but blue collar workers wouldn't buy products with a yuppie image. Physicians and investment bankers would buy Harley-Davidsons and pickup trucks, yet a lot of blue collar workers would be loath to drive Volvos or to drink bottled water, both of which they would consider unacceptably effete ("designer water" being a typically derisive term).

The issue was not one of cost, but of image. I knew a bricklayer who had season tickets to Blues hockey games, a comparatively pricey indulgence. While he would never buy a Ralph Lauren shirt, he would happily shell out a lot more for a Blues replica jersey. He wouldn't think of buying a Volvo or a Saab, but would unhesitatingly spend more money on a Dodge

Ram pickup or a bass boat. Our challenge was to give Schlafly Beer credibility with this bricklayer and others like him. We concluded that it would be easier to appeal to working-class consumers without alienating professionals than vice-versa.

We acknowledged that there were those who regarded beer from microbreweries as "designer beer," just as Evian was derided as "designer water." The purveyors of such products were seen as duping consumers into paying exorbitant prices for something that wasn't any better than the more reasonably priced mainstream version. We therefore made the conscious decision to position Schlafly as a traditional beer for everyone, not as a drink primarily for pretentious, overeducated elitists. We adopted the slogan "Beer the way it used to be" as a means of underscoring this message.

In addition to being an effective marketing tool, the phrase had the advantage of being true. By and large, the styles of beer we have chosen to brew have been around for more than 100 years and, in some instances, a lot longer. Moreover, we have adhered to the *Reinheitsgebot* (the Bavarian beer purity law) in brewing them. We have neither the inclination nor the capability to compete with the major breweries on such battlegrounds as purging as many carbohydrates as possible from every 12-ounce serving of beer.

The packaging for our bottled beer was chosen to reinforce the fact that we were offering beer the way it truly used to be. The bottles themselves were brown longnecks with caps that didn't twist off, but had to be removed with an opener. We replaced the Swiss ibex with a logo that recalled the halcyon days immediately following the repeal of Prohibition. The team at Core scoured old magazines to find the colors and script most reminiscent of a bygone era. We wanted every aspect of the package to remind consumers that we were offering beers that the mainstream breweries were no longer interested in making.

Ten years later, I think it's fair to say that this approach has worked. While we still occupy a small niche in the St. Louis beer market, and an even smaller niche in the surrounding region, we have generally been accepted across a pretty broad cross-section of the population. One sign of this acceptance, about which I have very mixed emotions, was something I saw on a bicycle ride in 2000: a Schlafly bottle lying in a gutter at the corner of Compton and Locust Streets in midtown St. Louis. On the one hand, as an ardent champion of city living, I abhor littering and denounce those who engage in it. At the same time, I felt a regrettable but very real sense of satisfaction that we had reached even this ignoble segment of the market. I must confess to having the same mixed reaction whenever I see a Schlafly bottle in a parking lot, near a bus stop or elsewhere in the urban landscape. That having been said, I would contend strenuously and defensively that my very unscientific surveys have consistently shown that our share of littered beer packaging is far lower than our share of sales (which is in itself a very small percentage).

Deciding to call our beer Schlafly still left unanswered the question of what to call the dozens of different styles we brewed. For the most part we have stayed with generic descriptions. Schlafly Pale Ale, Schlafly Oatmeal Stout, Schlafly Hefeweizen and Schlafly Pilsner were our first beers to be offered year-round in bottles and are all universally recognized styles. Pale Ale, which is approximately the color of iced tea, and thus darker than most American beers, is so named because it's paler than the opaque black and brown ales that were common in Britain when the style was developed. Oatmeal Stout is an example of one such dark ale. *Hefeweizen* is a German word to describe a wheat beer from which the yeast has not been filtered out. And Pilsner is the style that was created in the city of Pilsen, in what is now the Czech Republic.

Our thinking has usually been that coming up with our own clever names for our beers ran the risk of making them even more incomprehensible to a lot of consumers. Most Americans find it hard enough to know the differences among Altbier, Bock, Dortmunder, Porter, Scottish Ale and Weissbier (all long-established styles) without having to decipher the unique names that some breweries bestow on their versions of these beers. I have often had the experience of visiting a brewpub for the first time and finding myself unable to decode the menu and determine what styles of beer are, in fact, being offered. So, for the most part, we have chosen to name our beers for widely recognized styles.

That is not to say, however, that we have been rigidly scrupulous in our observance of this rule, especially in our early days. For example, we called our first Christmas beer Ebenezer's Holiday Ale in honor of Ebenezer Scrooge, the famous curmudgeon in *A Christmas Carol*, by Charles Dickens. Because some barley wines (very strong ales with alcohol levels that sometimes approach those of wines) incorporate the word "old" in their names (Old Nick, Old Foghorn), we called our first batch of barley wine Old Possum in honor of T. S. Eliot, whose childhood home was three blocks west of The Tap Room on Locust Street and who wrote the classic *Old Possum's Book of Practical Cats*, on which the musical *Cats* is based. Noting that most Bavarian Doppelbocks (very strong lagers) have names that end in "ator" (Salvator, Maximator, Animator, Triumphator, Fortunator, Optimator), we experimented with calling our Doppelbock "See ya later" and, more seriously, Illuminator.

The name that was perhaps our most whimsical came about when one of our brewers mistakenly used an ale yeast instead of a lager yeast while intending to brew a batch of Pilsner. Not wanting to dump 15 barrels (465 gallons) of beer, we decided to offer the brew that he produced as a cream ale, which we dubbed Pyrite Cream Ale, pyrite being a yellow mineral commonly known as "fools' gold." What better name for a golden ale that was the result of a foolish mistake?

The name that brought us the greatest amount of media attention was the one we selected for the beer that we brewed in honor of Pope John Paul II when he visited St. Louis in January, 1999. When the papal visit was first announced, we figured this was such an historic event that we needed to come up with a special beer to commemorate it. Not only was St. Louis the only city in the United States the Pope was planning to visit on his trip to North America, but his motorcade was scheduled to pass by our brewery several times.

We wanted to brew a beer that was characteristic of the Pope's native Poland and we took inspiration from a possibly apocryphal anecdote involving Pope Clement X, who early in his career had served as an auditor in the papal nunciature in Poland. On his deathbed, in Rome in 1676, Pope Clement is said to have cried out, "O, Santa Piva di Polonia!" Those around him thought the Pope was proclaiming a new Saint Piva from Poland, not realizing that he was actually asking for a Polish beer, *Piwo* being the Polish word for beer. While I cannot vouch for the historical accuracy of this account, I can absolutely confirm that it reassured us in our conviction that the incumbent Polish pontiff must be a beer drinker.

The problem with brewing an authentic Polish beer for the Polish pope was that the most popular style of beer in the papal homeland was Pilsner and we already brewed Pilsner. We also considered brewing a Baltic porter, a style popular in Lithuania and Poland and a variation on the more common English porter. But again, we already brewed a porter (a dark ale lighter in body than a stout) and we thought that Baltic porter wasn't sufficiently different from English Porter to be perceived as distinctive by most of our clientele.

We finally decided to brew a smoked porter, a widely recognized style that would be noticeably different from a conventional porter. The fact that it wasn't necessarily characteristic of Poland wasn't going to deter us. The Polish town of Grodzisk was renowned for its wood-smoked beer. It didn't matter that this beer wasn't a porter. Poles brewed and drank porter and they brewed and drank smoked beer. Who was to say they wouldn't drink smoked porter if given the opportunity? For the first time ever, a pope was coming to St. Louis, and we needed to start brewing.

Because the pope is properly referred to as His Holiness, the name we chose for the beer—possibly with the aid of divine inspiration—was Holy Smoke Papal Porter. It's safe to say that nothing we have ever done in the history of the brewery has generated publicity on the same scale as the media frenzy that surrounded this beer. Media outlets from all over the United States, including at least one from as far away as Alaska, wanted to cover the story. We got calls from television stations in Mexico, which the pope visited before coming to St. Louis. People from all over the country were inquiring how they could get the beer. Demand at The Tap Room was so high that we had to stop serving it weeks before the pope arrived, in order to ensure that we had an adequate supply while he was in town.

This enthusiastic reception prompted us to add smoked porter to our annual rotation of seasonal beers the following year. Stylistically, our brewers had done a good job and, like all of our seasonals, smoked porter had its coterie of loyal devotees. Nevertheless, absent the name Holy Smoke Papal Porter and absent all the hype that accompanied the pope's visit, the very same beer that had been an international sensation has never since come anywhere close to being the most popular style on our menu, even during the relatively short time it's available each year.

Therefore, in response to the query posed by Juliet over four centuries ago, I note:

What's in a name? That which we called Holy Smoke Papal Porter
By any other name might smell as good and taste the same,
But it sure as hell won't sell as well.

A TALE OF TWO CITIES

St. Louis, Missouri and Cologne, Germany have a lot in common. First, there's geography. St. Louis, which is on the west bank of the Mississippi, is the most important city on the most important river in North America. Cologne, which is on the west bank of the Rhine, is the most important city on the most important river in Europe.

Next, there's history. Both cities were part of the Napoleonic empire. It was Napoleon who sold St. Louis, along with the rest of the Louisiana Territory, to the United States in 1803. And it was Napoleon who assigned numbers to all of the houses in Cologne in 1796. He gave the number 4711 to the perfume factory owned by Wilhelm Muelhens, thereby helping to create a brand that has thrived for more than two centuries: 4711, *Eau de Cologne*.

Next, there's art. It's ironic that one of the best collections of 20th-century American artists can be found in the Museum Ludwig in Cologne, which features works by Andy Warhol, Jasper Johns and Roy Lichtenstein, among others; and the best collection in the world of works by the 20th-century German Artist Max Beckmann is at the St. Louis Art Museum.

Finally, there's music. The common theme of rings is found in the most famous musical works respectively associated with St. Louis and the Rhineland near Cologne. *St. Louis Blues* by W. C. Handy describes the prototypical St. Louis woman "with her diamond ring." And Richard Wagner's *Das Rheingold*, one of four operas comprising *Der Ring des Nibelungen*, is all about a magic ring made from a stash of gold at the bottom of the Rhine.

Given all these parallels between Cologne and my hometown, it may have been kismet that I was going to wind up with a Frau from Cologne. If it was, it certainly didn't happen overnight. By the time I was in my thirties, my mother was becoming a little impatient with my bachelor status. To quote from the opening line of *A Tale of Two Cities*, by Charles Dickens, "It was the best of times, it was the worst of times."

Without reaching the questions of whether I was being bad or good, or whether I was having too good a time, my mother was of the opinion that enough was enough. I still remember coming home in July of 1981 and hearing this message on my answering machine: "Tom, this is your mother calling. I wanted to let you know that Prince Charles is getting married tomorrow. He's your age and his wedding is tomorrow. In case you haven't read the news in the paper, heard it on the radio or seen it on television, I thought this was something you needed to know. That's all. Again, this is your mother." Ironically, it was the brewery, a venture about which my mother had been lukewarm, to say the least, that set in motion the series of events that eventually led to my tying the knot.

Shortly after opening the brewery, I decided it would be fun to learn German. I had always enjoyed languages, without ever becoming terribly proficient, and thought it would be appropriate for an aspiring beer baron to have at least some conversational fluency in German. In the fall of 1993, I signed up for a class that met one night per week at Meramec Community College and supplemented what I learned in the classroom by listening to tapes while I was driving.

A few months later, I went to a Christmas party at the Missouri Botanical Garden and overheard two women speaking in German. They were talking about other people at the party, confident that no one within earshot could understand what they were saying. By this time, I had learned enough German in class and from tapes to walk up and ask, "Entschuldigen Sie bitte, sind Sie Deutsche?" (Excuse me, are you German?) Ulrike was either totally charmed by this clever line or else was unable to get away, because she was on crutches from a skiing accident. For whatever reason, we ended up chatting, almost entirely in English.

I was thrilled to learn that Ulrike was from Cologne, which had dozens of breweries when she was growing up. I was then astonished to find out that she had drunk only one beer in her entire life. Granted, the Rhineland was renowned for its wine and she knew a lot about wines, but still. I found it totally inconceivable that someone could grow up around all those breweries without drinking more than one seven-ounce glass of one of their beers. It was as if someone from Florida had never tasted orange juice.

Ulrike's lack of interest in beer led to an awkward moment on one of our early dates. We were at her apartment and she had opened a bottle of wine. Then she said, "Oh, you have a brewery. Perhaps you'd like a beer." When I said I would, she began rummaging around in the back of her refrigerator until she finally produced a single can of light beer whose born-on date was undoubtedly years earlier. I politely noted that five-year-old wine was better than five-year-old light beer and asked her to pour me a glass from the bottle she had just opened.

Apart from her predilection for wine and mine for beer, there were other differences. For one thing, I'm much more verbal, while Ulrike is far more visual. Even though it's she who speaks three languages fluently (German, French and English), I'm the one who likes words and writing. She, on the other hand, has an artistic eye of which I'm in awe. She notices details and nuances in painting, architecture and garden design that completely elude me.

There was one difference of opinion that was potentially divisive: our different views of dogs. Ulrike, who had been bitten by a German Shepherd as a child, had been uncomfortable around dogs ever since. When we started dating, my constant companion of more than six years was a Chesapeake Bay Retriever named Sparky, whose picture is on the wall at The Tap Room. It was Ulrike's brother Carl who, upon hearing about Sparky, told her, "Don't tell Tom he has to choose between the dog and you. If you're going to fall in love with Tom, you're going to have to learn to love Sparky, because he's part of the package." To Ulrike's credit, she followed Carl's advice.

Of course, Carl may have had an ulterior motive in encouraging our romance. Like her other two brothers, when he heard we were dating, he said something to the effect of, "He has a brewery? Marry him." As straightforward as this sentiment might seem, when Carl came to St. Louis for a visit, I quickly discovered that his attitude wasn't quite so simple.

We were having dinner at The Tap Room and I pointed to the list of 10 or so beers currently on tap. Carl marveled at the variety and then scowled at one of the selections. "Warum hast Du Altbier?" he demanded. (Why do you have Altbier?) I explained that we prided ourselves on offering a wide selection of beers and Altbier (a copper-colored German ale) was a style from the Rhineland, not far from his home in Cologne. I had already said too much.

Carl said he knew exactly what Altbier was. It was the slop that came from Düsseldorf and he wasn't about to put it in his mouth. There is an intense rivalry between Cologne and Düsseldorf (which are only about 25 miles apart) that goes back to the Thirty Years War, if not earlier. Over the course of the next few days, Carl tasted every beer on the list except Altbier. He adamantly refused to have anything to do with Düsseldorf, including its beer. Cologne might have a lot in common with St. Louis on the other side of the Atlantic, but with Düsseldorf, just downstream on the

Rhine, *gar nichts!* (Absolutely nothing!)

Ulrike and I announced our engagement on Memorial Day, 1995, and scheduled the wedding for Labor Day weekend, a little more than three months later. We chose The Tap Room as the place to hold our reception, a choice that completely bewildered her mother. "You're going to have your wedding reception in a brewery?" It was almost as if we were going to have it in a factory or a coal mine. My traditional German mother-in-law couldn't begin to understand why Americans would have a wedding reception in an industrial facility like a brewery.

The wedding itself was at the St. Louis Cathedral at the corner of Lindell and Newstead in the Central West End. When we were designing the invitations, I thought we ought to list the address of the Cathedral. Ulrike vigorously disagreed, contending that it was totally inappropriate and unnecessary to list the address of a cathedral, citing Notre Dame in Paris and Cologne Cathedral as examples. I pointed out that there were several cathedrals in St. Louis, including the so-called Old Cathedral by the Gateway Arch, the so-called New Cathedral, where we were being married, and Christ Church Episcopal Cathedral. If we didn't want to cause confusion for our guests, many of whom were coming from out of town, we needed to list the address. I lost the argument.

On September 2, 1995, we were married in the same cathedral in which my great-grandfather William C. McBride's funeral had been held 78 years earlier. Our flower girl was Christina Valentine, the great-granddaughter of August A. Busch, Sr., who had been an honorary pallbearer at this funeral. After we had walked down the aisle together and reached the door to the church, Ulrike said we needed to go outside. I demurred, pointing out that it was hot outside; I was wearing a warm Austrian Loden jacket, and the church was comfortably air conditioned. Ulrike finally persuaded me that it was worthwhile to go out into the midday heat. She was right.

When we came out of the church, I saw the first surprise of our marriage: a giant cuckoo clock on a float that was the stage for the Waterloo German Band, musicians in Lederhosen and Dirndls playing German oompah music. We climbed onto the float with the rest of the wedding party and traveled to The Tap Room in style, toasting our marriage with Schlafly Beer from a keg on the float. Along the way, we passed some gentlemen sitting on the curb drinking something other than Schlafly from a container inside a brown paper bag. One of them caught the spirit of the occasion and raised the paper bag in salute, calling, "Yo, there goes Miss Germany." Ulrike gloried in her new title until I reminded her that she was now Frau Deutschland, i.e., Mrs. Germany.

To our surprise, there were quite a few guests at The Tap Room when we arrived. Some of them seemed much more surprised than we were and asked, "So, you went through with it?" "What do you mean?" "So, you actually did get married?" "Of course we did. Look at the wedding rings on our fingers." "But they told us the wedding had been canceled." "Who told you?" "The people at the church."

It turned out that some people had gone to the Old Cathedral instead of the New Cathedral and had seen that the parking lot was empty. When an official at the door asked why they were there, they said they were there for the wedding. Which wedding? The noon wedding. Didn't they know that the noon wedding had been canceled? Apparently not. Our guests then proceeded to The Tap Room anyway, figuring that I might back out of the marriage, but I surely wouldn't cancel a party. (I note for the record that this mistake would not have been made if we had put the address of the Cathedral on the invitation, as I had suggested.)

We left the reception in a 1957 Thunderbird, which had been generously lent to us by Lotsie Hermann Holton, another great-granddaughter of August Busch, Sr. There was, however, an element of mischief in her kindness. Tied to the back of the car were about a dozen Budweiser cans, which noisily trailed us all the way home.

We went to Switzerland for our honeymoon and spent the first night in Steinhof, the village where August Schlafly had been born. In conversing with some very distant cousins, I had great difficulty understanding their Swiss-German dialect. Even Ulrike had trouble understanding them. Curiously, they had much less difficulty with my High German spoken with an American accent.

The experience of being welcomed as family in Europe has been one of the benefits of marrying a woman from Germany. Even though my German is passable, at best, I have been accepted by Ulrike's friends and family in a way that would never have been possible if I weren't married to a native. The same thing is true on our side of the Atlantic. We have been pleased to host quite a few German visitors who would never have found their way to St. Louis if they weren't friends or relatives of Ulrike.

Among the Cologne connections we have maintained is a friendship with Heinrich Becker, one of the managing partners of the Privatbrauerei Gaffel, which brews Gaffel Kölsch, one of the most popular beers in Cologne. Heinrich has tasted and approved our Kölsch (a light ale characteristic of Cologne), a high compliment indeed, given the pride that residents of Cologne take in their hometown beer. And, on one occasion, he invited me to walk in the Karneval parade in Cologne with the owners of other local breweries. He is also an art aficionado with a magnificent collection of historic beer posters, some of which date from the 19th century. Ulrike and I arranged to have this collection shown in St. Louis in 2000. Copies of some of the posters from the collection are still on display at The Tap Room.

In order to accommodate the friends and relatives in Europe who were not able to travel to St. Louis for our wedding, we had what I persisted in calling a re-enactment (actually a renewal of vows) in Cologne on June 8, 1996. The ceremony was held in the Cologne Cathedral. We didn't list the address on the invitation. And, as far as I know, no one went to the wrong church. Along with all of our guests, we then took a *Bimmelbahn* (small train) from the church to the Rhine, stopping along the way at Brauhaus Sion, a famous brewpub. We then boarded a boat that would take us to Rodenkirchen, a suburb slightly to the south. The reception was at Zum Treppchen, a charming restaurant where former St. Louisan Tina Turner, who was then living in Cologne, had hosted a party one week earlier. We had to travel upriver to get there.

I was then reminded that, for all the many similarities between Cologne and St. Louis, the Rhine and the Mississippi flow in opposite directions. That's one of the many things that continue to make our marriage interesting.

THE IGNOBLE EXPERIMENT

A great social and economic experiment,
noble in motive and far-reaching in purpose.

Thus did Herbert Hoover describe Prohibition in a letter on February 28, 1928, to William E. Borah, a United States Senator from Idaho.

The prohibitionist movement in America predates the founding of the United States. Cotton Mather, the fiery Boston preacher who helped to instigate the notorious Salem Witch Trials in 1692, wrote in *Magnalia Christi Americana* (The Ecclesiastical History of New England), "Ale-Houses are Hell-Houses." Nearly two centuries later, during the campaign leading up to the presidential election of 1884, Dr. Samuel D. Burchard, a staunch enemy of saloons, denounced Democrats (the party of Grover Cleveland) as "the party whose antecedents have been rum, Romanism and rebellion." By contrast, of Republicans (the party of Cleveland's opponent, James G. Blaine) Burchard said, "We are loyal to our flag." The implication, of course, was that patrons of saloons were inherently unpatriotic, in addition to all their other moral failings.

The entry by the United States into the First World War in 1917 added fuel to the prohibitionist fire. The argument was made that raw materials and labor that were needed for the war effort were being diverted to brewing and distilling. More inflammatory was the anti-German rhetoric that was employed in favor of Prohibition. Pro-Germanism was condemned as the froth from the German's beer saloon. Prohibition was hailed as an infallible chaser of German submarines. The fact that major breweries bore such distinctly German names as Anheuser, Busch, Pabst and Schlitz helped to demonize beer even further.

It was in this climate that the 18th Amendment to the United States Constitution was drafted and approved by Congress. On January 8, 1918, Mississippi became the first state to ratify the amendment. On January 16, 1919, two months after the armistice that ended the war, Nebraska became the 36th state to ratify, thereby completing the process of making the prohibition of alcoholic beverages part of our national constitution. By the end of February, 1919, every state except Connecticut, New Jersey and Rhode Island had approved the 18th Amendment.

On October 28, 1919, Congress enacted the Volstead Act, the legislation implementing the 18th Amendment, the provisions of which officially took effect on January 17, 1920. Prohibition was the law of the land for nearly 14 years, until December 5, 1933, when Congress officially repealed the 18th Amendment by adopting the 21st Amendment, which had been introduced in February of 1933 and had received approval from the requisite number of states in less than nine months. Meanwhile, Congress had already legalized the sale of some beer by amending the Volstead Act's definition of "intoxicating liquors" to exclude beer with an alcohol content not exceeding 3.2 percent by weight. This statute took effect on April 7, 1933, the date we have commemorated in our annual festival celebrating repeal.

It should first be noted that there were a lot of people who were not as sanguine about Prohibition as Herbert Hoover was, including a lot of folks in Maplewood, where Schlafly Bottleworks is now located. On Saturday, February 18, 1922, Gus O. Nations, the chief prohibition enforcement officer in the district that included Maplewood, led five assistants on a raid of a saloon operated by Henry Kraemer at 7343 Manchester Road, slightly west of where Bottleworks is now. When the patrons of the saloon objected, a fight broke out, and Douglas Baker, one of Nations's assistants, shot Kraemer in the leg. As a result, a St. Louis County justice of the peace issued a warrant against Baker for assault with intent to kill.

That's right. Apparently, Prohibition was so unpopular at the time that St. Louis County filed charges against a so-called "dry agent" who fired his gun while enforcing the Volstead Act. According to contemporary news accounts provided to me by the Maplewood Historical Society, the warrant was issued following a conference among Justice of the Peace Stucker, Prosecuting Attorney Fred Mueller and Chief of Police Brown of Maplewood. The warrant was sworn to by Henry Kraemer Jr., son of the proprietor of the saloon. There was no report of any action taken against the proprietor of the saloon or any of its customers.

A second important point to note about the "noble experiment" of Prohibition is that it had some pretty ignoble supporters, including the Ku Klux Klan, whose bigotry was not confined to brewers of German ancestry. Enforcing Prohibition was a cornerstone of the Klan's agenda, with bootleggers, African-Americans, Jews and Catholics all regarded as threats to the hate group's vision of America. As a result, there was a great overlap in membership between the KKK and such groups as the Anti-Saloon League and the Women's Christian Temperance Union. For example, Edward Young Clarke, an Imperial Wizard and Giant Wizard of the Klan in the 1920s, was an ardent supporter of the Anti-Saloon League. And Daisy Douglas Barr, the Imperial Empress of the Women's Ku Klux Klan in Indiana in the 1920s, was an active member of the Women's Christian Temperance Union who died in a traffic accident on her way to a WCTU meeting in 1938.

In light of this historical link between the Ku Klux Klan and support for Prohibition in the 1920s, it's interesting that Senator Robert Byrd from West Virginia—whose loathing for alcoholic beverages has prompted him to denounce alcohol as "tobacco's evil twin"—is, as far as I know, the only former Klansman currently serving in either house of the United States Congress. Although Byrd claims to have severed his ties with the Klan when he was in his mid-20s, he subsequently wrote a letter to the Imperial Wizard in which he said, "The Klan is needed today as never before and I am anxious to see its rebirth here in West Virginia" and "in every state in the Union."

After supposedly leaving the Klan, Byrd vigorously opposed desegregating the armed forces, vowing that he would never fight "with a Negro by my side. Rather I should die a thousand times and see Old Glory trampled in the dirt never to rise again, than to see this beloved land of ours become degraded by race mongrels, a throwback to the blackest specimen from the wilds." He opposed the nominations to the Supreme Court of the only two African-American justices (nominated by presidents of two different parties) and took part in a filibuster against the landmark Civil Rights Act of 1964. To those who would contend that what Byrd might have said or done decades ago is irrelevant, I would note that, as recently as 2001, the statesman who condemned alcohol as "tobacco's evil twin" deliberately used an ugly racial slur on network television. Appearing on Fox News Sunday, Byrd twice used the hateful "N" word and proved it was not an inadvertent slip of the tongue by then saying, "I'm going to use that word."

Fortunately, mainstream public opinion now has little tolerance for such blatant bigotry as that expressed by Byrd, even though West Virginians continue to re-elect him and Senate Democrats continue to reward him with the perks of seniority. It is, however, still quite socially acceptable in some circles to vilify alcoholic beverages with rhetoric reminiscent of the 1920s and the alliances between the Ku Klux Klan and prohibitionist groups, notwithstanding the fact that these beverages have been legal since 1933.

I was brought face to face with this attitude in 2005 at a meeting of the Board of Directors of the St. Louis Public Library. One of the librarians told me she had been looking for information about "Art Outside," a fair for local artists held at Schlafly Bottleworks. Her search was thwarted, however, because a filter on the library computer had blocked access to the brewery's Web site. The reason was the Children's Internet Protection Act, which cuts off federal aid to public libraries that don't install appropriate filters on library computers. As a brewery, we were lumped together with child pornographers and hate groups in having our Web site blocked along with theirs. According to the librarian to whom I spoke, computers in most public libraries in the United States now have filters that block access to brewery Web sites.

I also encountered a disappointing manifestation of neo-prohibitionism at Georgetown University, my alma mater, which now houses the Center on Alcohol Marketing and Youth. CAMY, it should be noted, landed at Georgetown because the neo-prohibitionist Robert Wood Johnson Foundation shelled out $5 million to put it there. While the university's Web site boasts of its "intellectual openness," CAMY's modus operandi is anything but intellectually open. Rather, all of its sponsored research seems to start with the premise that advertising and marketing alcoholic beverages are ipso facto reprehensible. Data are then gathered to support this conclusion. The purportedly unbiased studies almost invariably recommend two solutions to the myriad problems that they have uncovered through their exhaustive inquiries: higher taxes on alcoholic beverages and greater censorship of advertising.

Typical of the evidence cited by CAMY to prove beyond a shadow of a doubt that advertising is aimed at children is the use of cartoons. According to CAMY and its allies, such as the Center for Science in the Public Interest, cartoons are deliberately intended to appeal to a youthful audience and not to adults. In view of the extensive advertising campaign by MetLife featuring Snoopy, I therefore suppose I should be grateful for CAMY's insights and the research it's conducting at my alma mater. Without these scholarly efforts, I might never have realized that MetLife was really trying to sell life insurance to teenagers.

On the political front in Missouri, I don't want to overlook State Senator Bill Alter from High Ridge, who, in January of 2006, introduced a bill that would have prohibited grocery stores and convenience stores from selling beer refrigerated below 60 degrees Fahrenheit. Ignoring the fact that beer keeps better when it's refrigerated (and for that very reason the labels on our bottles advise retailers and consumers to "keep refrigerated"), Alter claimed that requiring that beer be stored under less than optimal conditions would discourage drunk driving. Most interestingly, when a reporter for the *St. Louis Post-Dispatch* questioned Alter about one of the provisions in his bill, he referred all questions to Kristen Bogert, an 11-year-old fifth grader at Cedar Hill Intermediate School in House Springs, Missouri, whom Alter described as the real author of the bill.

When I read this account in the newspaper, I thought about calling Senator Alter and putting him in touch with CAMY. He could undoubtedly make the case that if an 11-year-old is capable of drafting legislation for the Missouri General Assembly, surely a 20-year-old is mature enough to watch a beer commercial on television.

Bill Alter isn't the only elected official in Missouri who hasn't looked kindly on alcoholic beverages. During the eight years that John Ashcroft served as governor of Missouri, he banned smoking, dancing and alcoholic beverages at the Governor's Mansion in Jefferson City. Knowing that Ashcroft would be leaving office in January of 1993, I had the idea of making Schlafly the first beer served in the Governor's Mansion since Christopher Bond had left office in 1985. Part of my motivation was the bragging rights that such a milestone would confer. But I also wanted to raise the profile of our beer in the state capital prior to the legislative session I discussed in Chapter 4.

Through a lawyer in my office who had close contacts with the staff of Governor-elect Mel Carnahan, I arranged to donate beer for the party that would be held in the Governor's Mansion after the official ball following his inauguration. On the afternoon before the party, our assistant brewer, Stephen Hale, and I drove from St. Louis to Jefferson City in a blizzard, with the kegs in the back of my Jeep Cherokee. A lot of dignitaries were in attendance, and our beer was well received. Four months later, the legislation we wanted was passed by the General Assembly and promptly signed by the governor. From the political perspective at least, our mission was accomplished.

But the best stories to come out of the evening had nothing to do with lobbying or the legislative process. In order to appreciate them fully, it's important to know that Missouri state troopers served the same role for the governor as the Secret Service does for the president of the United States, and that a lot of the work around the Governor's Mansion was performed by trusted convicts from the nearby state penitentiary.

Stephen and I arrived at the Mansion while the official inaugural ball was still going on. After setting up the jockey box from which we would serve the beer, we had a fair amount of time to chat with both troopers and convicts before guests began to arrive. We discovered that the Missouri state troopers, like the Arkansas state troopers who had attended Bill Clinton, were in a position to learn a lot of details about the Governor's private life. While the stories we heard about the Ashcroft family weren't nearly as bawdy as those told by Arkansas state troopers about Clinton, they were every bit as unflattering.

When Governor Carnahan arrived after his inaugural ball, I realized that he, having moved in only a few hours earlier, was at that point probably less familiar with the Governor's Mansion and its staff than Stephen and I were. When I introduced myself and started explaining how honored we were to be serving Schlafly Beer, it suddenly occurred to me that he had initially mistaken the two of us for convicts assigned to the Mansion.

For the first 10 years of Schlafly Beer, the prohibitionist attitudes I encountered tended to be generic. Critics were opposed to beer and other alcoholic beverages in general, not to us in particular. Because we were so comparatively small, we didn't catch anywhere near the amount of flak that Anheuser-Busch did. This situation changed dramatically in 2001, when we began to look seriously at Maplewood as the site for our second brewery. While the Maplewood city administration, its Chamber of Commerce and most of the local residents and businesses were overwhelmingly supportive, a nearby private school was overtly hostile to our opening a brewery in its neighborhood.

Frankly, the vigorous opposition from Metropolitan School took us completely by surprise. As I explained in at least one public forum and in meetings with the school's faculty, administrators, board members and parents of students, we had absolutely no interest in marketing or selling beer to their students. Our employees were trained to spot fake IDs; and, in our

10 years of operating The Tap Room, we had never been accused of selling to minors. I also pointed out that there were already quite a few bars and restaurants within a few blocks of the school. I gave strong assurances that we would be at least as vigilant as any establishment in Maplewood when it came to keeping beer away from underage drinkers. Finally, I noted that the building we intended to occupy had formerly been a supermarket, which would have sold a lot more beer, wine and spirits out the door than we ever would. We planned to sell draft beer in our restaurant and a limited number of six packs and kegs from our retail shop. But the overwhelming majority of what we planned to brew on the site, at least 90 percent, would be loaded onto trucks for sale to wholesalers. There was no way that the school's students, or any other member of the general public, could have access to this beer except at other retail accounts, most of which were miles away.

It was at this point that I learned that the school's professed concern was not with us as a retail account that might not have adequate safeguards against sales to minors. Rather, it was our mere existence as a brewery that was troubling. We were told that students from Metropolitan School were at risk when it came to alcohol. Allowing them to see a brewery near their school would compromise the school's educational mission. It didn't matter that we didn't target youth in our marketing or advertising. We shouldn't even be allowed to exist in a location where young people might see us.

In its efforts to keep us out of Maplewood, Metropolitan School employed a number of different tactics, ranging from letter-writing campaigns, to engaging the services of a powerful lobbyist in Jefferson City to block our being licensed, to sending a lawyer to oppose us in front of the Maplewood City Council. I can still recall the lawyer's shrieking, "Kegs! Kegs!" at one such meeting of the City Council, as if nothing more heinous could be imagined.

In the end, community support for us in Maplewood was much stronger than for Metropolitan School. The city approved the purchase of our building—in fact facilitated it—and issued all the necessary licenses and permits, as did St. Louis County and the State of Missouri. As for problems with Metropolitan School, the only incident of note took place when one of the students vandalized our construction site prior to our opening. I got a call from the executive director of the school, who told me that I would soon be receiving an apology from the student and his parents. Four years later, I'm still waiting for the promised apology.

MENS SANA IN CORPORE SANO

In wine there is wisdom. In beer there is strength. In water there is bacteria.

This slogan can be found on T-shirts at countless beer festivals all over the world and on lots of websites popular among beer aficionados. More often than not it's described as an "Old German proverb." While I applaud both the science and the sentiment expressed by the slogan, I must confess to having both a quibble and some doubts.

My quibble is grammatical and relatively minor. "Bacteria" is a plural word, the singular of which is "bacterium." A correct translation of the purported German proverb would have said, "In water there *are* bacteria," not "there is bacteria." My doubts, on the other hand, are more substantive and relate to the ascribed origins of the saying.

It's undeniably true that scientists have known about bacteria since the 17th century, when Antonie van Leeuwenhoek (whose mother came from a family of brewers, incidentally) discovered them with a microscope. But it was not until the 19th century, 200 years later, that Louis Pasteur discovered that boiling a liquid killed the germs within it. He thus developed the process known as pasteurization, which has wide application in both brewing and wine making. In short, I'm somewhat skeptical that it was old German folklore that produced an aphorism based on science that wasn't widely known and accepted until the late 19th century.

Whatever the provenance of the slogan, its underlying message— i.e., that it's safer to drink beer and wine than water—is nothing new. More than 1,900 years ago, the Apostle Paul wrote in his first letter to Timothy, "Drink no longer water, but take a little wine for the sake of thy stomach." He gave this advice along with several other recommendations for physical and spiritual health, the spirit of which would be consistent with the words of the Roman satirist Juvenal, "Orandum est ut sit mens sana in corpore sano." (One should pray for a healthy mind in a healthy body.) Recognizing that wine was good for the mind (*mens*) as well as the body (*corpus*), the Roman poet Horace wrote more than 2,000 years ago to Maecenas, "Nulla placere diu nec vivere carmina possunt / Quae scribuntur aquae potoribus." (No poems can please for long or live that are written by water drinkers.)

More than 1,500 years after Paul advised Timothy to drink wine for the sake of his health, Thaddeus Hajek was serving in Prague as the personal physician to the Holy Roman Emperor Rudolph II. In this capacity, in 1585 he published what is generally regarded as the first encyclopedic study of brewing. While some of Hajek's science is now discredited, e.g., his theories about alchemy and astrology, it's noteworthy that such a prominent physician and respected scientist devoted such an extensive scholarly treatise to the subject of beer.

While the science of 400 years ago might seem rather primitive by today's standards, it was already well known at the time that drinking beer posed less of a threat to one's health than drinking water, just as Paul had earlier counseled Timothy to drink wine instead of water. As I mentioned at the beginning of Chapter 1, the reason the *Mayflower* landed at Plymouth in 1620, two decades after Hajek's death, was that the supply of beer on board the ship was running low. Without understanding the underlying microbiology, the Pilgrims simply knew that those who drank water were more susceptible to illness than those who drank beer. The Pilgrims could not have known, of course, what we now know, i.e., that boiling water to brew beer kills germs, and alcohol and the acidity in beer and wine provide a hostile environment for germs.

It's not just the absence of bacteria that makes beer such a healthful beverage. There's also the presence of a lot of vitamins, especially from the B complex. As reported in the July, 2001, issue of the *European Journal of Clinical Nutrition*, Dr. O. Mayer, Jr., at Charles University in the Czech Republic, conducted a study in which his colleagues and he measured blood levels of vitamins B-6 (pyridoxine), B-9 (folate, which is also found in leafy green vegetables) and B-12 (cobalamin). The researchers focused on these vitamins because they were found in beer and were thought to lower blood levels of homocysteine, a compound associated with increased risk of heart disease. Dr. Mayer's study of residents of the town of Pilsen, which has one of the highest per capita rates of beer consumption in the world, showed that drinking beer regularly for three weeks led to increased levels of these three B vitamins and decreased levels of homocysteine.

In addition to the nutrients found in most beers, dark beers also contain a lot of flavonoids, which are polyphenolic compounds also found in red wine, chocolate and many fruits and vegetables. Flavonoids are important because they act as anti-oxidants and help to prevent atherosclerosis (hardening of the arteries) and other heart diseases, along with such neurodegenerative diseases as Alzheimer's and Parkinson's. Scientists have also reported antiviral, anti-allergic, anti-platelet and anti-tumor activities by flavonoids.

Even hops contain an important nutrient or, more precisely, a micronutrient, known as xanthohumol. This is a compound, first discovered in 1913, whose anti-cancer properties were studied at Oregon State University in the 1990s. Researchers at OSU's Linus Pauling Institute found that xanthohumol, which helps to detoxify some carcinogens and inhibit tumor growth, could be effective against breast, colon, ovarian and prostate cancers.

In addition to the salubrious qualities that are unique to beer and wine, all alcoholic beverages can have salutary effects on the health of moderate drinkers. For example, a study of diabetic men conducted by Dr. Mihaela Tanasescu at the Harvard School of Public Health found an inverse correlation between the risk of heart disease and the consumption of alcohol. As reported by Reuters, "Compared with nondrinkers, men who consumed a half drink or less per day cut their heart disease risk by 24 percent, while those who drank one-half to two drinks per day cut their risk by 36 percent. And men who drank more than two drinks per day had a 41 percent lower risk of heart disease."

Scientific studies have also demonstrated what the poet Horace knew intuitively, i.e., that drinking alcohol can, in fact, sharpen the mind. As reported in the *American Journal of Epidemiology* in 2004, Sir Michael Marmot, a professor of epidemiology and public health at University College, London, gave psychometric tests to more than 6,000 civil servants. The tests measured short-term memory, mathematical reasoning and verbal skills. Test results were then matched with drinking habits.

According to the London *Telegraph*, "those having even a single glass of wine a week scored significantly higher in the tests than more abstemious drinkers. Teetotalers were twice as likely as occasional drinkers to achieve the lowest scores." The *Telegraph* goes on to report, "Those who downed the equivalent of half a bottle of wine or two pints of beer a day scored best of all. The effects were apparent even after the results had been adjusted to take into account such factors as physical and mental health." (It's worth noting that a British pint is 20 ounces, meaning that the most intelligent group in the study drank, on average, the equivalent of three and a third 12-ounce bottles of beer per day.)

Much of the benefit of beer comes from its role as a social catalyst. While scientists have spent a lot of time on studies documenting the role that anti-oxidants play in increasing blood flow to the brain, thereby enhancing the mental capacity of the beer drinker, we at Schlafly have always been much more interested in how beer promotes socialization. It would be my contention that the interesting conversations that often take place over pints of beer are at least as beneficial to the brain as enhanced blood flow.

It would also be my contention that most beer drinkers agree with me. I am constantly mindful that customers in bars and restaurants willingly pay nearly three times as much for a glass of beer as the same amount of beer would cost in a supermarket. Considering that they could be drinking the same beer at home for nearly two-thirds less, what do bars and restaurants offer that's worth such a premium?

Having overheard and taken part in a lot of conversations over many years with patrons of a number of different establishments, including our own, I am certain that it's the stimulating conversations with others that lead them to pay the premium for drinking beer at a bar or restaurant as opposed to their own living rooms. The fact that these conversations are, by definition, interactive means that the patrons exercise their brains in ways that they wouldn't by reading or watching TV at home.

A good example of this process at work was the 2006 World Cup soccer matches, which attracted sizeable crowds at our bars even when the United States wasn't playing. For a number of reasons, the clientele interested in World Cup soccer has tended to be somewhat more cosmopolitan than stereotypical sports fans. I am convinced that one of the main reasons they chose to watch World Cup games without sound at The Tap Room or Bottleworks, and not in their homes, was the opportunity to commune with kindred spirits, who might very well be staunch supporters of opposing teams. The chance to talk to other cognoscenti about a game that isn't universally appreciated or understood in the United States had significant appeal.

This is not to say that televised soccer, popular though it may have been, has been the most cerebral offering at either of our locations. Regular programs at Bottleworks have included a film series sponsored by Webster University, a monthly theology forum and Science on Tap, which features professors from Washington University. At The Tap Room, we have hosted Theology on Tap, sponsored by the Aquinas Institute of Theology, and

numerous programs of the American Council on Germany, featuring am-
bassadors and other distinguished speakers. Through these and countless
other events, Schlafly Beer has helped to create or nurture communities
with common intellectual interests.

We have also been involved in sports beyond simply spectating. A
number of us at the brewery have collectively finished marathons in several
cities in the United States and Europe. Speaking only for myself, one of
the best parts of training for the New York Marathon in 1994 was continu-
ally replenishing my carbohydrates, of which beer was an excellent source.
As a company, we included a five-kilometer run as part of our Oktoberfest
celebration; sponsored the Spirit of St. Louis Marathon; sponsored a soccer
team; and sponsored the Sunday Morning Rugby Club. Among our more
unusual sponsorships has been the annual Scottish Games in Forest Park.

While I have never tried to throw a caber in the Scottish Games, I
did participate in one sporting event we sponsored in which I was as much
overmatched as if I had gone head to head with some burly Highlanders. In
1996, I entered a mountain bike race, co-sponsored by Schlafly Beer and a
local bicycle shop. As a recreational cyclist who had done a fair amount of
riding on off-road trails, I thought I was up for the event, even though I had
no illusions of winning.

When the organizers announced that some of the course was "a
little technical," alarms should have gone off in my head. I also should have
taken note when I realized that I recognized a lot of the other contestants
as bicycle messengers whom I had seen jumping curbs and dodging buses
in the streets of downtown St. Louis. I also should have been tipped off by
overhearing their discussions of the prize money offered at various other
mountain bike races.

My collision with reality came about one minute into the race,
when I encountered a large tree that had fallen across the trail. While I
dismounted and prepared to hoist my bike over the tree, all the other rac-
ers were jumping over it like thoroughbreds in a steeplechase. Whoever
finished second to last was considerably ahead of me. It was, however, quite
gratifying to see all these superior athletes enjoying their Schlafly Beer
when I finally wobbled across the finish line.

Despite the many health benefits of drinking wine or beer, talking about them is extremely controversial, as some wineries discovered in

1999. On February 5 of that year, the Bureau of Alcohol, Tobacco and Firearms approved two statements for wine labels. One, which had been proposed by a California vintner, said, "The proud people who make this wine encourage you to consult your family doctor about the health effects of wine consumption." The other, which had been sought by the Wine Institute, said, "To learn the health effects of wine consumption, send for the Federal Government's Dietary Guidelines for Americans." It then listed the address of the Agriculture Department's Center for Nutrition Policy and Promotion.

The notion that wineries might be allowed to refer people to their family physicians or to published federal guidelines was totally unacceptable to Senator Robert Byrd from West Virginia. It was this action by the BATF that inspired the former Klansman to denounce alcohol as "tobacco's evil twin." Interestingly, Byrd's biggest ally in the Senate in this battle was Strom Thurmond, who also had a long history of bigotry (along with a mixed-race child whom he had not yet publicly acknowledged).

Byrd and Thurmond were joined in the fray by Barrett Duke, the Vice President for Research and Director of the Research Institute of the Ethics & Religious Liberty Commission of the Southern Baptist Convention. Duke, the former pastor of the Cornerstone Baptist Church in Denver, vigorously opposed the wine labels and characterized the wineries as purveyors of "snake oil."

Upon reading this reference to snake oil, I was reminded of fundamentalists who handle poisonous snakes because they think the Gospel of Mark tells them to do so; but for some reason they don't drink wine, even though the advice from the Apostle Paul on this point is far more explicit than Mark's purported instructions to handle snakes. Given a choice between Biblical injunctions to drink wine or handle rattlesnakes, I know which one I'd choose to follow.

I then wondered what Dr. Duke would say about a wine label that told consumers to read Paul's letter to Timothy. Would he consider the Apostle Paul a snake oil salesman for writing that there were health benefits from drinking wine?

IN CEREVISIA VERITAS

The truth is a precious commodity. That's why I use it so sparingly.

This quotation has been attributed to Mark Twain by the late Senator Sam Ervin among others; and, for all I know, Twain actually said it, or something like it. Although I haven't been able to track down where or when he supposedly said it, this certainly sounds like something that Twain could have said or written.

Mark Twain's presumed cynicism notwithstanding, the truth has always enjoyed an iconic status in almost every civilization throughout history. Twenty-five hundred years ago, Confucius said, "The aim of the superior man is truth." Approximately 140 years later, Plato wrote, "Truth is the beginning of every good thing, both in heaven and on earth." Today the seal of Harvard University contains the single word *Veritas* (which is Latin for Truth), while the seal of its rival, Yale, bears the phrase *Lux et Veritas* (Light and Truth).

Even before Confucius made his famous observations, societies had recognized that fermented beverages were a source of truth. When Pliny the Elder coined the proverb *In vino veritas* (In wine there is truth), he was repeating a sentiment that had been expressed 650 years earlier by the Greek poet Alcaeus, "Wine, dear boy, and truth."

As for the phrase *In cerevisia veritas* (In beer there is truth), having taken Latin for seven years, from seventh grade through my freshman year in college, and having taught first-year Latin, I had sufficient knowledge of the language to be able to plug the Latin word for beer into Pliny's proverb. As I soon discovered, however, I was by no means the first pseudo-classical scholar to do so. As far as I can tell—and I must admit to not having researched the point all that thoroughly—no ancient Roman ever actually wrote the phrase down on anything that has survived to this day; and a lot of other modern-day beer lovers have had enough of a classical education to be able to find the word *cerevisia* in an English-Latin dictionary and know how to use the ablative case.

However murky or recent its origins might be, there is still a great deal of wisdom in this aphorism. First, and most obviously, it describes the propensity of people to speak honestly and truthfully after drinking beer. But it also connotes something slightly more subtle, namely, authenticity. Beer is a beverage without artifice or pretense. Beer is inherently trustworthy because it stands for getting back to basics.

While some might regard it as both pompous and self-contradictory to spend time philosophizing about a drink that purports to be straight-forward and easily approachable, this discussion really goes to the heart of what makes us who we are as a brewery. At Schlafly we are philosophically committed to authenticity with every beer we brew. If we say we're going to make a particular style of beer, that's what we make, and we follow the guidelines for the style to the best of our abilities. As George Washington said in his *Farewell Address* in 1796, we "hold the maxim no less applicable to public than to private affairs, that honesty is always the best policy." Apparently, however, not every brewery feels as we do.

One need look no further than the label for Miller Lite, which bears the description "True Pilsner Beer." It doesn't simply claim to be a Pilsner, but a *True* Pilsner, the quintessential exemplar of the style. The only problem is that Miller Lite doesn't even come close to meeting the standards of a true Pilsner. The Pilsner style originated in the town of Pilsen, in what is now the Czech Republic. A true Pilsner is one that faithfully adheres to the standards of this style. Beers that have been purged of calories and carbohydrates are, by definition, not true to the style. Miller Lite might very well be an excellent rendition of some style of beer; and that style, whatever it might be, is probably related to Pilsners. But no one would ever mistake Miller Lite for the Pilsners that are found in Prague.

I also find a source of puzzlement in the beer whose label features a picture of Samuel Adams along with the text: "Samuel Adams Boston Lager — Once small brewers like Samuel Adams crafted full-bodied distinctive American beers. Americans have since lost the true taste of great beer. Now the Boston Beer Company brings back craft-brewed beer." So, what's my problem? Yes, Samuel Adams, who signed the Declaration of Independence, was from Boston and brewed beer. And yes, Boston Beer Company now makes some very good beers.

My problem is with the implication that Samuel Adams was even familiar with a beer like Boston Lager, much less brewed anything that even remotely resembled it. As a lawyer and a former English major, I'm capable of dissecting the syntax of what's written on the label and readily acknowledge that there is technically nothing untruthful. That having been said, the label certainly gives the impression that Boston Lager is somehow reminiscent of the beers produced in Samuel Adams's brewery. After saying that Samuel Adams "crafted full-bodied distinctive American beers," the label then says, "Boston Beer Company brings back craft-brewed beer." The average reader could easily be led to conclude that Boston Lager, or something like it, was once crafted by Samuel Adams and has now been brought back and named for him.

Such a conclusion, reasonable though it might be, would be totally erroneous. Samuel Adams died at least 35 years before lager beer was brewed in America—that is, if Adam Lemp did, in fact, make a lager as early as 1838. Given that lager beer was unknown in Boston during Samuel Adams's lifetime, I'm not sure what kind of craftsmanship is being brought back. It's a little like claiming to bring back the craftsmanship of the traditional 19th-century television. Just as the first television wasn't produced until well into the 20th century, there was no such thing as lager beer in Boston until long after Samuel Adams had gone to his eternal reward.

The wording on a label from another brewery in St. Louis isn't so much misleading as curious: "This is the famous Budweiser beer. We know of no brand produced by any other brewer which costs so much to brew and age." Really? What about Grolsch, Redhook and Widmer for starters? According to an Anheuser-Busch press release from February 21, 2006, announcing an agreement with a large Dutch brewery, A-B is now "the U.S. importer of the upscale Grolsch traditional European beer brands." Redhook and Widmer, both of which are based in the Pacific Northwest, are described on an Anheuser-Busch website as "Alliance Partners," meaning that A-B is a partial owner of each and offers the brands through its distribution system.

Upscale, it should be understood, is a synonym for more expensive. What Grolsch, Redhook and Widmer have in common, in addition to their alliances with Anheuser-Busch, is that they generally sell for considerably more than "the famous Budweiser beer." Yet, according to the Budweiser label, these brands produced by other brewers don't cost as much to brew and age. If these other brands are less expensive to brew than Budweiser, why don't they cost less in supermarkets? It's not that I have any basis whatsoever for questioning the veracity of the Budweiser label. It's more that I marvel at A-B's ability to command higher prices for brands that it says are cheaper to make.

I also marvel at some of the neologisms coined by some of the major breweries, one of my favorites being "packaged-draft" beer. Leading the pack in this regard is Miller, which offers Miller Genuine Draft in bottles and cans. Not content with the simple oxymoron of offering "packaged-draft" beer, like others in the industry, Miller goes even further by calling its bottled and canned brews *Genuine Draft*. This characterization is as egregious as the claim that Miller Lite is a *True Pilsner*.

For the record, *Webster's New Universal Unabridged Dictionary* defines "draft beer" in a way that would be understood and accepted by most Americans: "beer drawn or available to be drawn from a cask or barrel." According to the same dictionary, this usage can be traced to 1780-90. The idea that draft beer comes in a can or bottle is simply inaccurate. The notion that bottled or canned beer is Genuine Draft is totally preposterous. It's like saying that frozen orange juice is freshly squeezed.

This is not to say, however, that draft beer is necessarily superior to packaged beer. Consider the poem "In a Prominent Bar in Secaucus One Day" by X. J. Kennedy, wherein a patron who is now down and out describes her once elegant lifestyle:

Once the toast of the Biltmore, the belle of the Taft,
I would drink bottle beer at the Drake, never draft.

If this lady were reincarnated today, she would probably be as amazed as I am by the Orwellian characterization of canned beer as somehow flowing from a tap at a bar.

By contrast, we have always strived to be scrupulously forthright in labeling our beers. Our Pilsner, for example, follows the specifications for the Pilsners brewed in the Czech Republic. Our Expedition Reserve American Pale Ale, which we brewed to commemorate the Lewis and Clark expedition, was comparable to the ales that would have been brewed in 1804, albeit with much different technology. Our 1904 American Lager, which we brewed to commemorate the St. Louis World's Fair, was very similar to the beers that fairgoers would have been drinking.

Whatever we and other breweries might say about ourselves, I have learned over the years that what others say about us carries much more credibility with the general public. Having been bombarded with advertising since their infancy, most consumers have a healthy skepticism with regard to most commercial messages. What the independent media say, on the other hand, carries a lot more weight. Even more persuasive are the opinions of respected peers. If the critics pan a movie, advertising by the studio usually won't save it at the box office. And the opinions of friends can generally trump the movie critics.

For the past four years, the readers of *Sauce Magazine*, a guide to food, drink and living in St. Louis, have voted Schlafly the best local brewery. This recognition has meant a lot more than our simply proclaiming ourselves the best. Likewise, favorable reviews on Web sites frequented by beer aficionados have a big advantage over paid endorsements when it comes to the perception of sincerity.

Actually, we have enjoyed very good media relations from the very beginning. The idea that someone would even think of opening a brewery in the backyard of Anheuser-Busch was newsworthy in and of itself. As a result, we got a lot more attention than a small business like ours would otherwise warrant. We have also benefited from what I call the "herd instinct" among journalists. If one local TV station plans to cover one of our events, more often than not the others will follow, so as not to be left out. Fortunately for us, the coverage has been almost invariably positive.

Initially, a lot of the stories emphasized the David and Goliath aspect of our status next to Anheuser-Busch. I remember talking to an employee of a public relations agency that did a lot of work for A-B, who was frustrated that his client was being "beaten up in the media." I assured him that his client's treatment in the media was no reflection on his professional skills, which were considerable. Rather, it was a phenomenon that was both predictable and inevitable. There was no way a newspaper would ever report that I was picking on his client. In the case of any disagreement between the two largest breweries in St. Louis, his client would always be the bad guy, no matter what the facts were and no matter how he spun them.

While we haven't completely shed our role as David to Anheuser-Busch's Goliath, I think it's fair to say that, over time, A-B, to the extent it pays any attention at all to us, has come to regard us more as an ally than an adversary in the area of media relations. On several occasions, public affairs people at the larger brewery have realized that we can be a much more sympathetic face for the industry than they are. Thus, when I was preparing to write a letter to the newspaper in opposition to a proposed increase in the beer excise tax, Anheuser-Busch supplied me with data to help make the case. The people there recognized that the argument was more persuasive coming from a small, independent, local business than from a multinational giant. And it was in their self-interest that the data I cited were accurate.

As for what the media say about us, as opposed to what we say in the media, I've learned some useful lessons over the years. Some are quite obvious. Not only does a news story have more credibility than paid advertising; it's also a lot cheaper. There's no way we could afford to buy three minutes of television commercials during prime time. To have an objective voice say something positive about us during the evening news is a double whammy. We could never afford to pay to put such a message on the air, and it's a lot more believable precisely because the viewers know we didn't pay for it.

I've also learned that getting exposure in the media requires more than passively waiting for stories to appear. It helps to look at things from the perspective of the reporters and the editors and producers for whom they work. Every day they need to fill a certain number of column inches in the newspaper or a certain number of minutes in the TV or radio news broadcasts. The reporters have the additional motivation of wanting their stories to be the ones deemed newsworthy by their editors or producers. The easier we make it for journalists to do their jobs, the more likely they are to include us in their stories.

This is not to say that journalists can be manipulated. They have a lot more experience interviewing sources for stories than I have being interviewed. And there's no better way to antagonize a reporter than to try to dictate what he or she should say. Nevertheless, I've found out that I can increase the likelihood of media coverage by doing something as simple as returning calls promptly. Reporters work on deadlines. If I call back promptly, we have a better chance of being mentioned in a story. If I have a reputation for returning calls promptly, I'm more likely to be called first by a reporter who has a deadline looming and needs a quote from someone in the beer business.

In addition to being accessible to reporters, it's even more important to be reliable. Dan Kopman, who keeps his ear to the ground for what's going on in the world of beer, has been the source for a number of stories that had nothing to do with Schlafly. Over the years, business reporters have learned that they can depend on Dan's insights and general sense of which trends are leading in which direction.

There's also no reason to wait to be called by the media. If something is newsworthy, I don't hesitate to call a reporter with whom I've established good relations. If I have a history of credibility, reporters are generally willing to listen to my explanation as to why something merits a story. And I'm always upfront about my reason for calling. Reporters are all sophisticated enough to know that I'm trying to generate free publicity. Instead of pretending that's not my reason for calling, I volunteer that that's exactly why I'm calling and then move on to the reasons why it's in their interest to cover the story. I have also called reporters to give them leads on stories that don't involve Schlafly in any way. While doing so doesn't result in any immediate publicity for us, it helps us to build a reputation for reliability with these reporters.

Of course, we can't always count on others to tell our story for us, persuasive though their opinions might be. From time to time, we have done some desultory advertising, sometimes on radio (including underwriting on community and public radio stations), sometimes in print and even on billboards. Sometimes the focus has been the beer brand in general, but more frequently it has been specific to a special event. As for our comprehensive advertising strategy, I'm not sure any of us could articulate it, or even if we've ever actually had one. As I said in Chapter 1, our history as a company has been more improvisational than orchestrated. This has absolutely been the case with respect to advertising.

One of our more consistent vehicles for telling our story has been *The Growler*, our monthly newsletter, which is disseminated both electronically and via regular mail. The name comes from what the *Oxford English Dictionary* defines as "a vessel in which beer is fetched." The fact that growling is a very elemental and visceral way of communicating made the name all the more appealing to us. A typical issue includes a calendar of upcoming events, a listing of seasonal beers, photographs of fans wearing Schlafly hats or shirts in various spots around the world, and my column, titled "Top Fermentation."

The ostensible reason for my writing the column is that it gives people another reason to read our newsletter. Presumably, those who spend an extra five or six minutes per month voluntarily reading our message, whatever it might be, are more likely to buy into the message and buy our beer. To that end, I always try to make the column interesting and entertaining. How successful I am in doing so is a periodic topic of discussion within the company and among our customers.

My real reason for writing the column is that I was an English major in college and always aspired to be a writer. Unfortunately, before starting the brewery, I was never able to get anything published. Owning a majority interest in the company that puts out *The Growler* solved this problem. Now I no longer have to worry about pleasing a publisher. *C'est moi.*

In addition to *The Growler*, I have also found other outlets for my urge to write, including this book, a project recommended by Dan Kopman, perhaps as a way to keep me occupied and out of his way so he could focus on running the brewery without interference on my part. One of the most fun projects has been the Courthouse Steps, a troupe of singing lawyers for whom I write lyrics. We specialize in song parodies that poke fun at just about everyone in the news. Among the most popular have been "Leader of Iraq" sung to the tune of "Leader of the Pack," "Al Qaeda" to the tune of "Elvira" and a timeless number about the Clinton White House, "The Pain and Strain Came Mainly from the Stain."

Even with the Courthouse Steps, who periodically perform at The Tap Room, I have found a way to promote our beer brand in one of the songs. The tune is that of "Toora Loora Looral," which was made famous in the movie *Going My Way*. The Courthouse Steps parody, which celebrates some of cuisine unique to St. Louis, includes the immortal lines:

> *Toasted ravioli, concretes from Ted Drewes,*
> *Bags of belly-bombers, washed down with Schlafly brews.*

It's enough to make Bing Crosby turn over in his grave.

I have another outlet on Burns Night, our annual celebration of the Scottish poet Robert Burns, who was born on January 25, 1759. With inspiration from Dan Kopman's Scottish wife, Sheena, the evening includes bagpipes, haggis, cock-a-leekie soup, Scotch Ale, patrons in kilts, readings from the works of Burns and my reading of a poem composed for the occasion. Ever since our first Burns Night in 1992, I've recited a poem about the return of the ghost of Robert Burns. Although I change the poem somewhat every year, some themes have been constant from the beginning:

From Glasgow to the Hebrides, when Scottish bagpipes wail
And drummers drum for Robert Burns, 'tis time to drink Scotch Ale.
'Tis the day when all of Scotland drinks to Robert Burns.
And if ye drink enough Scotch Ale, Old Robert's ghost returns.

His ghost returns resplendent with his sporran, tam and kilt.
And he's been known to curse in verse, should his Scotch Ale be spilt.
His kilt's the pride of Scotland. It bears the family tartan.
He wears nothing underneath. Burns's ghost is Spartan.

Although the ghost is somewhat shy, he just need lift a glass
Of Scotch Ale. Then he'll lift his kilt for every passing lass.
On Burns Night he eats haggis, Scotch eggs and cock-a-leekie,
While lassies lift the laddies' kilts to sneak a little peekie.

Several stanzas later, the poem ends with a toast:

Now I ask you all to join me in a toast
To the spirit of tonight, Robert Burns's ghost.
In his lifetime he enjoyed many pleasures without guilt.
Let's raise a glass to one who raised our spirits and his kilt.

Before I leave the topic of ghosts, there's one more point worth making about ghosts, *cerevisia* and *veritas*. Not one word of this book has been ghost written.

IN HEAVEN THERE IS NO BEER

A rabbi, a Catholic priest and an Episcopal priest went into a bar.
Although that sounds like the opening line of a joke, it's actually
the lead for our next story.

This was how popular television anchor Julius Hunter told St. Louis viewers about what happened at The Tap Room on September 17, 1998.

The occasion was the official opening of the north bar at The Saint Louis Brewery. As those who are familiar with the brewery know, it consists of two buildings with a common basement, connected by hallways on each floor above ground. We had originally opened in the south building, which had suffered less damage in the 1976 fire and was in much better condition. Whenever we were asked when we planned to renovate the north building, the answer was always "next year," which meant 1992, then 1993, then 1994, etc. After six years of procrastinating, we finally decided that it was time to do something. For one thing, we had to admit that the dilapidated north building—from the basement it was possible to see daylight through the roof of the three-story structure—was both an eyesore and a potential safety hazard. Second, we were finally comfortable that we had enough funds to proceed with the renovation.

As with a lot of our projects, people were working frantically until the last minute. With the opening ceremony scheduled for noon on September 17, the building wasn't ready to be inspected until that morning, at which point the necessary occupancy permit was issued. With television cameras already in the room, only minutes before the ceremony was about to begin, Stephen Hale, James Ottolini and others were still struggling to connect the beer lines through which the inaugural pints were about to flow.

The dedication, which began on time, completely blurred the separation of church and state. It was supposed to include an appearance by Mayor Clarence Harmon, whose office had picked a date when he would be available. After Harmon's late cancellation, Francis Slay, the President of the Board of Aldermen, stepped in and read the Mayoral Proclamation, declaring September 17, 1998 to be "The Saint Louis Brewery, Inc. Day" in the City of St. Louis. The opening also featured the blessing of the brewery by Rabbi Joe Rosenbloom from Temple Emmanuel, Father Christopher Hanson from the St. Louis Abbey, and Canon Cricket Cooper from Christ Church Cathedral.

This blessing was a great example of interfaith cooperation. The clergy agreed among themselves that they would speak in order of seniority of their respective creeds—Judaism, then Roman Catholicism, then Anglicanism. The theme of the day was religious harmony, with no evidence whatsoever of doctrinal bickering. Without directly acknowledging the famous polka song "In Heaven There Is No Beer," they all thanked heaven for the gift of beer—implicitly saying that there must be beer in heaven if that's where the beer on earth ultimately came from—and asked for God's blessing on our enterprise. While I don't recall the particular scripture readings, it's very possible that one of them was from *Psalms* 104, 14-15, which thanks God for "plants for us to use, so we can grow our crops and produce wine to make us happy." There may also have been a reading from *Deuteronomy* 14, 25-26, which instructs the Israelites, "Sell your produce and take the money with you to the one place of worship. Spend it on whatever you want—beef, lamb, wine, beer."

This event was so well received that we decided to do something similar when we opened the restaurant at Bottleworks in January of 2004. In addition to Mayor Mark Langston of Maplewood, we invited our neighbors, Dr. Brian Newcomb, the pastor of Christ Church, United Church of Christ, and Father Terry Niziolek, the pastor of Immaculate Conception Catholic Church, both of whom blessed our operation. We had invited pastors of other nearby churches to join in the blessing, but none was able to accept our invitation. Significantly, however, no congregation in Maplewood voiced any public objection to our opening, not even the two Baptist churches, despite the fact that some of their co-religionists have expressed overt hostility towards wineries, breweries and others who make or sell alcoholic beverages.

As I noted in Chapter 9, in 1999 Dr. Barrett Duke, speaking on behalf of the Southern Baptist Convention, denounced wineries as purveyors of "snake oil." More recently, in June of 2006, this same Southern Baptist Convention adopted the 57th resolution in its 161-year history, condemning alcohol. This latest resolution, titled "On Alcohol Use In America," said in part:

RESOLVED, That the messengers to the Southern Baptist Convention meeting in Greensboro, North Carolina, June 13-14, 2006, express our total opposition to the manufacturing, advertising, distribution, and consuming of alcoholic beverages; and be it further

> RESOLVED, *That we urge that no one be elected to serve as a trustee or member of any entity or committee of the Southern Baptist Convention that is a user of alcoholic beverages.*

> RESOLVED, *That we urge Southern Baptists to take an active role in supporting legislation that is intended to curb alcohol use in our communities and nation.*

It's worth noting that the SBC's opposition to breweries isn't limited to their primary business of brewing and selling beer. It even extends to the free distribution of safe drinking water to hurricane victims. Thus, after Hurricane Wilma struck Florida in October of 2005, the Alabama Baptist Convention State Board of Missions refused to distribute cans of water to hurricane victims in Clewiston, Florida. The reason? The 22 pallets of canned water had been donated by Anheuser-Busch and—worse yet —the company's logo was on the cans.

In all fairness, it should be made clear that the Alabama Baptist Convention is not necessarily representative of the entire denomination. It's part of the Southern Baptist Convention, which was formed in May of 1845 in Augusta, Georgia, largely because of a fundamental disagreement with northerners over the question of slavery. Prior to this split, Baptists' antipathy towards brewing, distilling and winemaking doesn't seem to have been as consistent and fierce as it has been from Southern Baptists since 1845.

For example, it was a Baptist minister named Elijah Craig who is credited by many with having invented bourbon whiskey. According to the conventional wisdom, he started distilling in Bourbon County, Kentucky, using corn in his mash, and thus invented the style of whiskey that was named for the county in which it was first made.

Others, however, have challenged Craig's status as the inventor of bourbon. Charles K. Cowdery, for example, has pointed out that when Bourbon County was carved out of the Kentucky District of Virginia—i.e., before Kentucky entered the Union on its own—there were already dozens or even hundreds of distillers in the region. Moreover, there are currently 34 counties in Kentucky that were once part of the original Bourbon County.

More to the point, says Cowdery, Craig built his first distillery in 1780 in Fayette County and never had a distilling operation in the larger, earlier Bourbon County, much less in the smaller, current one. Cowdery adds that the first whiskey to be made in what is now Kentucky was probably distilled in 1774 or 1775 in what was then Lincoln County (now Mercer County). In other words, Craig didn't make the first whiskey in Kentucky and never made whiskey in Bourbon County; nor was Bourbon County where the first whiskey in Kentucky was distilled.

Putting aside all the quibbling about who had the first distillery in Kentucky and where it was located, what is not disputed is that Elijah Craig, a respected Baptist minister, operated a distillery. He did so in a region that was subsequently dominated by Southern Baptists—after the split over slavery—and at a time when there apparently was minimal social opprobrium for doing so.

In addition, it should be emphasized that Elijah Craig, ordained minister and distiller, wasn't some kind of renegade but was very much in the mainstream of his denomination. In 1798, he founded the academy that later became Georgetown College in Georgetown, Kentucky (not to be confused with my alma mater in Washington, D.C.), the first Baptist college west of the Allegheny Mountains. Until November of 2005, this Georgetown College was officially affiliated with the Kentucky Baptist Convention, which is part of the Southern Baptist Convention.

On November 15, 1810, two years after the death of Elijah Craig, Matthew Vassar, who was only 18 years old at the time, took over the management of his family's brewery in Poughkeepsie, New York. Six months later, on May 10, 1811, the brewery was totally destroyed by fire. Matthew immediately began to rebuild the business, initially brewing three barrels of beer at a time. By the early1840s, Vassar's brewery had an annual production of 15,000 barrels, and the beer was distributed up and down the East Coast. By 1860, production had doubled to 30,000 barrels annually, making the brewery one of the largest in the nation.

What is noteworthy from today's perspective is that Matthew Vassar, like Elijah Craig, was a devout Baptist. According to his autobiography, he was a trustee of the Baptist Church in Poughkeepsie and donated between $25,000 and $30,000 for the construction of a new house of worship, a very substantial sum at the time. Vassar also had something else in common with

Craig. In 1861, he founded a college, the eponymously named Vassar Female College, which changed its name to Vassar College in 1867. For years, he was fondly remembered in a popular Vassar song:

And so you see, to old V. C.
Our love shall never fail.
Full well we know that all we owe
To Matthew Vassar's ale.

In the interest of political correctness, the words were later changed to:

And so you see, to old V. C.
Our love shall never fade.
Full well we know that all we owe
To Matthew Vassar's aid.

Actually, despite the stern resolutions emanating from the Southern Baptist Convention, and despite the supposed horror of some members of the Alabama Baptist Convention at handling cans of water bearing the logo of a brewery, there's reason to believe that the spirit of Elijah Craig and Matthew Vassar is alive and well in the Southern Baptist Convention today. According to the food and beverage manager of a hotel in downtown St. Louis, who wishes to remain anonymous, when the SBC had its annual meeting in St. Louis in June of 2002, business in the hotel bars was down, as might be expected, but sales from the mini-bars in the rooms were up. If what he says is correct, one might conclude that the messengers drank just as much as other conventioneers. They just didn't do so publicly.

It wasn't just the rabbi, the Catholic priest and the Episcopal priest who provided us with inspiration on September 17, 1998. We were also inspired by the Mayoral Proclamation. Now that September 17 had been officially proclaimed "The Saint Louis Brewery, Inc. Day" in the City of St. Louis, we thought, why not turn this into an annual celebration? The brainstorming that ensued led to our holding our first annual "Hop in the City" beer festival in 1999.

We had, of course, participated in a lot of beer festivals, some local, some as far away as Colorado, Pennsylvania and Wisconsin. Upon returning, our thoughts were always the same: Throughout the year we brew as many styles—then about three dozen—as are represented at these other festivals;

and, in a lot of instances, our beers are at least as good as, if not better than, the offerings of other breweries. Why don't we put on a festival featuring our own beers?

There was another constituency calling for us to stage our own beer festival: our customers. Of the many styles of beer we brew (now about 40), most are seasonals and are available only during certain times of year. These seasonal beers, however, all have ardent fans who beseech us to make their particular favorites available year-round. With our Hop in the City beer festival, we were able to respond to these demands. While we can't offer all 40 beers throughout the year, on one Saturday in September, every fan of every seasonal beer knows that his or her particular favorite will be available at Hop in the City.

The success over the years of Hop in the City, which we took outside St. Louis for the first time in 2005, gave us the confidence to put on other festivals. Thus, when the St. Louis Art Fair arbitrarily stopped selling Schlafly Beer, we knew what to do. If the organizers didn't want to sell our beer at their fair, fine. We'd put on our own art festival.

The St. Louis Art Fair, an annual event on the streets of Clayton, was at one time an ideal venue for Schlafly Beer. We reached our peak of popularity the year that patrons at the Art Fair consumed 66 kegs of our beer in a single weekend. At the time, Schlafly was offered at two concession stands and served in cups with our logo. The following year, we were told that the beer could only be sold at one stand and could not be served in cups with a Schlafly logo. This latter restriction was particularly damaging to sales, since a lot of business had been generated by patrons walking around with Schlafly cups, prompting others to ask where they had gotten the beer.

Later on, in 2002, after Schlafly had been well received at eight consecutive Art Fairs, we were told that our beer was no longer welcome. The initial reason given was that there wasn't time to get the necessary licenses. When I offered to get the licenses, I was told that the real reason was that the fair was consolidating its vendors and wanted to deal with fewer wholesalers. When I pointed out that the fair was continuing to buy wine from our wholesaler—meaning it could buy Schlafly without dealing with an additional wholesaler—I was given a revised explanation and told that the real reason was, in fact, that Schlafly wasn't sufficiently profitable. I then pointed out that a cup of Schlafly sold for four dollars, while a cup of Budweiser sold for three dollars. Considering that a cup of Schlafly, which cost the fair about 88 cents, sold for a dollar more than Budweiser, even if the fair got the Budweiser free of charge, the profit margin on a cup of Schlafly would still be higher.

I never was told why officials at the Art Fair abruptly refused to stop selling such a popular beer. I was, however, solemnly assured that the decision was totally unrelated to large donations to the fair from any other brewery or any of its wholesalers.

We soon learned that we weren't the only ones who felt excluded by the St. Louis Art Fair. A lot of local artists had become very frustrated at not being able to display their work at the Art Fair, which almost exclusively featured works by artists from out of town. So it was that "Art Outside" was launched at Schlafly Bottleworks in 2004. As the only brewery in St. Louis County, we had been bounced from an art fair held in the county seat. Who better than we to host a festival for St. Louis artists who were also not welcome?

Unlike the St. Louis Art Fair, the St. Louis Strassenfest has never allowed Schlafly to be sold. The event, which purports to be a German-style street festival, is held every year a few blocks from The Tap Room. For some reason, the organizers aren't interested in serving authentic, German-style beers brewed in the neighborhood, as would be the case at a real Strassenfest in Germany. Even more bizarre, the allegedly authentic festival has readily served rivers of Smirnoff Ice, which probably violates the *Reinheitsgebot* (German beer purity law) more egregiously than any other beverage on the planet. Also unlike the St. Louis Art Fair, the Strassenfest organizers have never told us why we're not welcome and have simply stonewalled our offers of sponsorship.

Whatever the motivation of the organizers, the outcome is the same. Schlafly Beer is just as unwelcome at the Strassenfest as it is at the Art Fair. Having learned from our Art Fair experience the futility of trying to insinuate ourselves into a festival where we're not welcome, we decided simply to do what had worked before and start our own event: hence, "Schlaffenfest," our annual "City Fair" to benefit KDHX, a community radio station in St Louis.

Of all the many festivals in which we've been involved, the one that stands out most in my mind is the Hop in the City held on September 15, 2001, four days after the infamous attacks known simply as 9/11. Like everyone else in the United States, we were in a state of shock. And we were utterly clueless about what to do. For months we had been gearing up for a beer festival, which suddenly seemed both trivial and inappropriate. What were we supposed to do? Cancel? Go ahead? There was obviously no written manual or anything in our collective experience that could give us any guidance.

After a lot of soul searching, we decided to proceed with the festival. Having seen endless replays of airplanes hitting the World Trade Center, I remember hearing a psychologist telling Americans to unplug their televisions. As a country we needed to shed our paralysis. The best way to show the terrorists they hadn't succeeded was to resume our normal daily lives.

But there was something more than simply going back to our daily routines. Our lives had been forever changed. In one sense, we had gained a greater appreciation for each other. We looked at total strangers with an increased awareness of our shared humanity. And we needed each other's company more than any of us would have admitted on September 10.

It was this last consideration that ultimately caused us to go ahead with Hop in the City. We thought that people needed to escape the isolation of their living rooms and commune with others. While a beer festival might not be the most sophisticated form of psychotherapy, we told ourselves that it would be good for the souls of those who felt like coming. Our instincts were absolutely right.

The crowd was the most respectful I have ever seen anywhere. People waited patiently in lines without any jostling and I did not hear any rude words exchanged among any of the 2,000 people in attendance. Even after a couple of hours, when beer festivals run the risk of becoming a little boisterous, the festival goers were extraordinarily mellow.

It was at this point that I went to the microphone to make a few remarks. Again, there was no precedent for what one is supposed to say at a beer festival in the wake of a national tragedy; but we all felt that we somehow had to acknowledge the events of the past week. I briefly explained our decision to go ahead with the festival. I expressed our collective gratitude for the freedom to enjoy occasions such as this. Then I asked for a moment of silence.

What happened next was stunning, humbling and edifying. A huge parking lot full of people who had been drinking beer for a while fell totally silent. And they remained silent. No one whispered to anyone else. No one tried to fill a glass. The stillness on that warm September afternoon was truly awesome. Not awesome in the sense of perfunctory praise, but awesome in the sense that the memory still fills me with awe. Pedestrians on the nearby sidewalk stopped to observe the silence along with us. Drivers on Locust Street stopped their cars and joined in our silence.

I realized that the silence would continue until I did something to end it, but I didn't feel like ending this wonderful mood that I knew I would never again experience at a beer festival. Finally, I gestured to the bagpipe band we had hired for the occasion, which began playing "Amazing Grace." Only after the final note did people resume talking and drinking; and only then did the cars on Locust Street continue on their way.

A few weeks later, Dan Kopman, who describes himself as a nice Jewish boy from Clayton, had the opportunity to speak to the congregation of Concordia Lutheran Church, whose parking lot adjoins that of Schlafly Bottleworks in Maplewood. At the time, we owned the building but had not yet started renovating it; and Dan was calling on all the nearby property owners to explain what we planned to do in the vacant supermarket and to answer any questions they might have. Given Martin Luther's well-known fondness for beer, Dan didn't anticipate any opposition from this particular audience. Then the following exchange took place:

"Are you really planning to brew beer right next to our church?"

"Yes, we are."

"And you're going to be selling beer right there?" (gesturing toward the empty building across the parking lot).

"That's correct."

"Are you planning to sell beer on Sunday?"

"Uh, yes. That's our plan" (thinking to himself, "Where is this going?")

"Well, are you going to have a TV so we can watch the Rams games after our services?"

At this point, Dan, the consummate salesman, knew he had closed the deal.

POOR RICHARD AND GENIAL BEN

Beer is living proof that God loves us and wants us to be happy.

This oft-quoted aphorism is one of many attributed to Benjamin Franklin. In it Franklin expresses a sentiment similar to what was said by the various clergy who blessed our two breweries and thanked God for all His many gifts, including good beer. Interestingly, Franklin, unlike the clergymen and clergywoman who blessed The Tap Room and Schlafly Bottleworks, did not belong to any religious denomination.

Benjamin Franklin was born in Boston, Massachusetts, on January 17, 1706 (January 6, 1705, under the old-style calendar, which was not changed until 1752). At the time, Boston was still very much under the influence of Cotton Mather, who, as was mentioned in Chapter 8, had denounced "Ale-Houses" as "Hell-Houses" and instigated the Salem Witch Trials.

As a young man, Franklin ran away from the intolerance of Mather's Boston and ended up in Philadelphia, the City of Brotherly Love. Here he found a prevailing climate of comparative tolerance, in which divers Christians and even Jews lived in relative harmony. After extended European sojourns, Franklin returned to Philadelphia in 1785. On the 4th of July, 1788, pursuant to his instructions, the celebratory parade included clergy of several Christian denominations and a rabbi, all walking arm in arm. At his funeral two years later, in 1790, Ben Franklin's coffin was accompanied to the cemetery by all the clergymen in Philadelphia, representing all the different creeds.

Ben Franklin, beloved by many in his lifetime, was a man of many interests and accomplishments. As a businessman, inventor, scientist, politician, philanthropist, diplomat and author—to name just some of his avocations—he is almost without peer. One is reminded of John F. Kennedy's observation that a gathering of 49 Nobel Prize winners represented the greatest collection of talent in one room except, perhaps, when Thomas Jefferson dined alone. I think a good case could be made that Franklin rivals Jefferson as a polymath.

Considering what an extraordinary person Benjamin Franklin was, it's not surprising that there would be a major commemoration of the tercentenary of his birth. Moreover, considering Franklin's fondness for beer, it's not at all surprising that American breweries would want to participate in this commemoration. And so it was that *Poor Richard's Ale* came to be brewed by more than 100 breweries and brewpubs nationwide.

The idea originated with the Brewers Association, a not-for-profit trade and educational association for craft brewers and home brewers. In October of 2005, the BA selected the recipe for the beer that would be brewed in honor of Ben Franklin. The name *Poor Richard's Ale* had been inspired by *Poor Richard's Almanack*, the composite name for the almanacs of adages published by Franklin from 1732 to 1757 under the pseudonym of Richard Saunders. The recipe, which was supposed to be authentic for Ben Franklin's era, incorporated both corn and molasses. These were ingredients favored by Franklin, who encouraged Americans to make more use of native foodstuffs, such as corn, to minimize their dependence on Britain.

Among the breweries that brewed *Poor Richard's Ale* were Anheuser-Busch and Schlafly. When I first heard about A-B's participation in the Ben Franklin commemoration, I wondered whether the decision makers at the other brewery were aware of Franklin's extremely unflattering comments about the bird that adorns their corporate logo:

> I wish the bald eagle had not been chosen as the representative of our
> country; he is a bird of bad moral character; like those among men
> who live by sharping and robbing, he is generally poor and very lousy.

Even more surprising than Anheuser-Busch's choosing to honor a man who had derided the company's hallowed corporate symbol was the story that appeared in the *St. Louis Post-Dispatch* on January 18, 2006, under the headline, "Local breweries lift toast to Ben Franklin" by Gregory Cancelada. As Cancelada put it:

> A Schlafly beer served at the St. Louis tour center of Anheuser-
> Busch Cos., the nation's largest brewer? Tom Schlafly, owner of the
> St. Louis Brewery, Inc., sipping an Anheuser-Busch product?
>
> These sights might cause people to do a double take, but that's what
> happened Tuesday afternoon, when staff from Anheuser-Busch and
> St. Louis Brewery, the maker of Schlafly beer, gathered to toast
> Benjamin Franklin's birthday.

The newspaper got it right. Schlafly and Anheuser-Busch had, in fact, come together to celebrate Ben Franklin's 300th birthday. We had toasted him with our respective versions of *Poor Richard's Ale*, which the brewers from both breweries agreed tasted remarkably alike. And we had done so for the shared purpose of promoting the image of beer. Given Franklin's appreciation for beer, his prowess as a diplomat and his demonstrated commitment to tolerance, who better than Genial Ben to unite us in pursuit of a common goal and in a toast to mutual prosperity?

It was over pints of our two breweries' *Poor Richard's Ale* that Dan Kopman and I started discussions with folks at Anheuser-Busch about jointly launching the St. Louis Brewers Heritage Festival, the first of which is due to be held in Forest Park in St. Louis in May of 2007.

The caliphs at One Busch Place were finally accepting our new religion.

INDEX